SOANE
AND
DEATH

The Tombs and Monuments of Sir John Soane

SOANE
AND
DEATH

Edited by Giles Waterfield

DULWICH PICTURE GALLERY

MCMXCVI

This catalogue accompanies an exhibition held at
Dulwich Picture Gallery, 29 February–12 May 1996

Contents

Foreword

Soane's designs for tombs and monuments constituted a small but important aspect of his work. They have received considerable attention in recent decades, but with the emphasis rather on the theme of the architect's preoccupation with death than on the theoretical context in which the designs were developed. The aim of the present exhibition is to assemble the relevant drawings, for the most part from Soane's own collection, in order to study the design process applied variously to modest tablets and to the most ambitious mausolea at St Pancras and Dulwich Picture Gallery; and in the catalogue to examine the monuments in the light of the work carried out recently on Soane, especially by David Watkin for his forthcoming edition of the lectures.

It was at an exhibition on the restoration of Soane's monuments organised by the Soane Monuments Trust at the RIBA in 1989 that the idea first emerged of mounting an exhibition, on the same theme but using original drawings, at Dulwich Picture Gallery. At Dulwich survives perhaps the most remarkable of these monuments, and it must form the central exhibit of the present display.

The Soane Monuments Trust was set up in 1987 with the aim of funding and implementing the restoration of Soane's monuments and tombs, several of which were at that time in a poor state of repair. Since then it has been instrumental in restoring a number of the monuments discussed in this catalogue. I have been much encouraged by the enthusiasm of the Trust under the chairmanship of Robin Moore Ede for this exhibition, and I am most grateful both for their financial support and for the valuable role played by Stefan Buzas, himself a trustee, in designing the installation. One of the achievements of the Trust has been the sponsorship of a research fellow, Ptolemy Dean, to make a register of Soane's

minor buildings (a category into which many of these monuments fall) and I am very pleased that it has been possible to include here examples of his work as a recording artist.

Although Soane's own monuments are now generally in good condition, the numerous other surviving outside tombs of the period have received much less attention than they deserve, and in many cases are in a state of advancing dereliction. One aim of this exhibition, particularly through Roger Bowdler's essay, is to draw attention to their plight and to encourage greater interest in their threatened future.

For financial help in mounting the exhibition, the Gallery is greatly in the debt of its Friends, who have once again provided generous and much-needed support. A further contribution has come from the Gallery's own Stanley Scott Fund (for exhibitions and publications). The exhibition could not, however, have been organised without an unsolicited and extremely handsome anonymous donation: if only the morning's post more often included such surprises.

Government Indemnity for the exhibition has been kindly arranged by Bettie Clark and her colleagues at the Museums and Galleries Commission.

We are much indebted to the trustees of Sir John Soane's Museum for the generosity of their loans. The staff of the Museum have been extraordinarily helpful in many ways, and it is a pleasure to acknowledge the assistance particularly of Helen Dorey, Susan Palmer, and Margaret Schuelein. I am very grateful to Christopher Woodward, Assistant Curator at the Museum, for his energetic and extremely valuable work in preparing the catalogue entries, and for the many suggestions he has made for the improvement of the exhibition. Peter Thornton gave much assistance during the early stages of preparation when he was Curator of the Museum. His successor, Margaret Richardson, has shown herself encouraging, helpful, wise, resourceful and accommodating throughout: I am greatly in her debt. The lenders to the exhibition have been most generous and helpful, and I would like particularly to acknowledge the help of John Keyworth and Tim Knox.

At Dulwich Picture Gallery I am most grateful to all my colleagues for their help in many different ways: particularly Stephen Atherton, Richard Beresford, Victoria Bethell, Alan Campbell, Sophie Chessum, Sheila Gair, Kate Knowles, Charles Leggatt, Tom Proctor, Lucy Till and Elizabeth Wedmore. Barry Viney has once again taken great care over the design of the catalogue, which has been printed by Lavenham Press with their usual efficient rapidity. The students in the Paper Conservation Department of Camberwell College of Arts played an important role in mounting the drawings under the guidance of David Collins.

This is the last exhibition that I shall organise at Dulwich as its Director. It seems appropriate to acknowledge my gratitude to all the colleagues with whom I have worked over the years in planning and implementing exhibitions. Most particularly I would like to express my debt both to the founders of the Gallery, whose tomb forms so important a feature of the present display, and to the new board of trustees chaired by Lord Sainsbury. Under this new board the Gallery has not only been reconstituted as a new charitable trust but in effect founded anew, allowing the original founders, we must hope, to sleep quietly for many more years in their mausoleum.

Giles Waterfield
Director, Dulwich Picture Gallery

David Watkin

Monuments and Mausolea in the Age of Enlightenment

'The paths of glory lead but to the grave'[1]

Soane's preoccupation with what Summerson appropriately described as 'the Furniture of Death' must be set in the context of his identification with the ambitions of Enlightenment thinkers and architects to return to origins. Tombs, dating from three or four thousand years before Christ, are the earliest surviving monuments in the history of western architecture. Investigation of the origins of architecture, so powerfully expressed in the eighteenth-century passion for archaeology, thus resulted in the discovery of innumerable artefacts associated with death: tombs, mausolea, sarcophagi, altars, cenotaphs, and cinerary urns. In every country in Europe in the second half of the eighteenth century, designs for sepulchral architecture flourished as never before: between the founding of the Royal Academy in London in 1768 and the year 1820, no less than 164 designs for mausolea and 'sepulchral chapels' were exhibited.[2] Soane was not unusual in his obsession with the mausoleum and the paraphernalia of death, but the constant recurrence of funereal themes in his own work goes beyond that of any of his contemporaries. This strand in his œuvre has often been interpreted as in some way related to his naturally melancholy and introspective disposition, his family disappointments and tragedies, and his sense of being persecuted and misunderstood.

Soane chose to illustrate his lectures on the history and theory of architecture at the Royal Academy with a vast range of ancient tombs and funerary monuments in Egypt, Persepolis, Corneto, Rome, Pompeii, Albano, Agrigentum, Ravenna, Saint Rémy, Tarragona, and, in modern Turkey, at Halicarnassus, Telmissus, and Mylassa.[3] One of the reasons for Soane's interest in such monuments was his realisation that they had provided ancient architects with wide scope for indulging in novel and experimental forms. In that respect they provided a parallel to the role played by garden buildings in the development of eighteenth-century architecture. Soane seems to have believed that the tremendous variety in both form and detail of antique mausolea undermined the widespread misunderstanding, implicit in authorities such as Vignola, that ancient architecture was governed by a set of rules. Soane was anxious to demonstrate the falsity of the view that, by following these supposed rules, the modern architect would produce buildings equal to those of the Ancients. He thus enjoyed teasing his pupils by showing them the so-called Tomb of Theron at Agrigentum, in Sicily, where, in violation of normal rules for the orders, Ionic columns are surmounted by a full Doric frieze with triglyphs and metopes. Soane also found that ancient tombs and mausolea were intriguing topics for study because Vitruvius, whom he frequently used as a guide, had nothing to say about their design.

No less important for Soane was his realisation that funerary monuments played a key role in the public life of the ancient world where, celebrating the actions of heroes, they performed a function which, in the modern world, was more usually played by the written word. The expression of civic virtue was one of the key preoccupations with the Enlightenment writers studied by Soane such as Lubersac[4] and Patte.[5] These had constantly held up the Ancients as model citizens, high-minded, public-spirited figures for whom all art was devoted to public not private good. Eighteenth-century writers were particularly impressed by the fact that the Ancients publicly honoured their dead by burying them on the roads leading into their cities. Soane was fully committed to the Enlightenment ambition of reviving this practice which seemed increasingly desirable as inner-city churches had become over-crowded and insanitary with countless monuments and interments.

Soane was aware, too, that ancient funerary monuments functioned not only as expressions of worldly power and virtue, as in the imperial mausolea of Augustus and Hadrian, but of religious belief, and especially of hope in life after death. Most ancient Romans believed in an afterlife, however shadowy: some, indeed, considered that it occupied a shady underground world. In accordance with his Enlightenment and Freemasonic sympathies, Soane had a sense of identity with the approach to death of the Ancients. An abstract Deist rather than a conventional Anglican, he consciously eschewed all Christian symbolism in his designs for monuments and mausolea. He chose instead to pepper them with pagan symbols of eternity, above all the serpent biting its own tail.

Any student of the topic of Soane and death must be indebted to the brilliant article by Sir John Summerson, to which an allusion has already been made, 'Sir John Soane and the Furniture of Death'.[6] Summerson emphasised how eighteenth-century architects found the mausoleum an ideal subject for the untrammelled exercise of the imagination since the dead do not need light or air. Also, the forms of the typical mausoleum such as cylinder or pyramid appealed to the love of elemental geometry which characterised the generation of 'neoclassical' architects who were seeking escape from 'baroque' ornament.

Summerson also outlined four phases through which Soane's obsession with the mausoleum, sarcophagus, and cinerary urn, passed chronologically. These began with his youthful studies for mausolea for James King and the Earl of

Fig. 1 The Breakfast Room, 13 Lincoln's Inn Fields

Chatham, theoretical essays which enabled him, like Chambers before him with his mausoleum for the Prince of Wales, to display his powers of composition; then there was an archaeological phase marked by the design of rooms resembling Roman tomb chambers, such as the Breakfast Room of 1792 at 13 Lincoln's Inn Fields (fig. 1), and the Breakfast Room of 1800 at Pitzhanger Manor, with its urn-filled columbaria, depicted by Gandy in a watercolour which heightened its funereal atmosphere; there then followed a period in which Soane was confronted with the task of designing actual places of burial, rich with the imagery of eternity, for Sir Francis Bourgeois in Charlotte Street and at Dulwich, and for his wife and his family in St Pancras churchyard; finally, in a return to his archaeological phase, he incorporated the Belzoni Sarcophagus into the crypt at Lincoln's Inn Fields and, in an act of 'senile antiquarianism', formed the Monk's Yard and tomb in an adjacent area.

Though helpful as an outline guide, this neat quadripartite development overlooks the broad context of the role of the mausoleum in Enlightenment thought as a vehicle for the expression of civic virtue and, no less significantly, as a means of expressing moods which were mysterious or sad. Soane studied a range of French eighteenth-century writers on architecture who stressed the affective role of architecture as an expression of appropriate character. Boffrand, Blondel, and Le Camus de Mézières cited the mausoleum as a building type appropriate for the expression of moods which were *'sérieux et triste'*. Boffrand's *Livre d'architecture* (1745) contained an essay entitled *Principes tirés de l'art poétique d'Horace*, which was one of the key texts of eighteenth-century architectural philosophy. Boffrand took a familiar classical text, the *Ars poetica* of Horace, and transferred from poetry to architecture its doctrine of appropriate character. Soane, who owned Boffrand's book and frequently studied Horace's *Ars poetica*, will have been struck by Boffrand's stress on the mausoleum. This appeared in Boffrand's commentary on the following passage in Horace:

> It is not enough that poems should have beauty; if they are to carry the audience with them, they must have charm as well. Just as smiling faces are turned on those who smile, so is sympathy shown with those who weep. If you want to move me to tears you must first feel grief yourself ... Pathetic language is appropriate to the face of sorrow, and violent language to the face of anger; a sportive diction goes with merry looks, and serious with grave looks. For nature has so formed us that we first feel inwardly any change in our fortunes.[7]

Transferring these principles to architecture, Boffrand wrote,

> It is not enough for a building to be beautiful, it must be agreeable, and enable the spectator to feel the character which it must communicate in such a manner that it is cheerful to those to whom it should communicate joy, and serious and sad to those to whom it should communicate respect or sadness.

> If one wishes to make a music room or salon for the reception of company, it must be cheerful by its disposition, brightness, and the manner in which it is decorated. If one wishes to make a mausoleum, the building must be treated appropriately to its subject and with a type of architecture and decoration which must be serious and sad; for nature makes our heart susceptible to these different impressions and it is always stirred by their union.[8]

Boffrand was followed by Burke's seminal essay of 1757 on the aesthetic of the Sublime which influenced Blondel and Le Camus de Mézières who, in 1780, stressed how architecture could express emotions of gaiety, majesty, and sadness.[9] Echoing Boffrand's language, Le Camus described how light could be handled to make interiors *'mystérieux ou triste'*, words which Soane copied out in the course of his lengthy translation of Le Camus' book.[10] The climax of this tradition was reached with the designs and theories of Etienne-Louis Boullée (1728–99) who conceived a new expressive architecture of shadows. Sadly, Soane cannot have known the work of Boullée who was obsessed, like Soane, with the expression of appropriate character in architecture. Boullée, however, went beyond Soane in believing that funerary architecture offered the architect the greatest scope for the creation of what he, like Soane, called the poetry of architecture.

We should now turn to the other tradition we have noted, that of the mausoleum or monument as moral exemplar. The ancient Romans believed that their distant ancestors had buried their honoured dead in the precincts of town houses. This custom, echoed in modern times by Soane's patron Sir Francis Bourgeois, had long been prohibited in ancient Rome where it had been replaced by tombs lining the roads leading into great cities, almost like a series of modern

Fig. 2 Soane, lecture illustration after Piranesi, *Via Appia, Rome* (SM)

advertisement hoardings. The idea, particularly as expressed in the numerous surviving monuments along the Via Appia in Rome, captured the imagination of eighteenth-century writers and artists, notably Piranesi, one of whose stunningly evocative images of the Via Appia was copied by Soane for use as a lecture illustration (fig. 2).[11]

The rationalist thinkers of the eighteenth century were attracted by the ancient custom of lining roads with monuments rather than cluttering up the interiors of churches with them, as in the modern world. No writer was more decisive on this point than Soane's favourite theorist, the Abbé Laugier, Part V of whose *Observations sur l'architecture* (1765) was entitled, 'Monuments to the Honour of Great Men'. In it, he urged not only that monuments and mausolea should no longer be suffered in churches, but also that they should be erected to the memory only of great, and not of

obscure, men. Emphasising that 'mausolea offer a rich field for the imagination of artists',[12] Laugier pointed as examples to ancient Roman examples in southern France such as the avenue of marble tombs forming the approach to Arles, and the monuments at St.-Rémy which Soane illustrated in his Royal Academy lectures.

Laugier's message was taken up by Jacques-François Blondel, the greatest architectural educator in eighteenth-century Europe. Soane spent much time in translating large sections of the first volume of Blondel's *Cours d'architecture* (9 vols., 1771–7), while in the second volume he would have found a section dedicated to cemeteries. Recommending that cemeteries should be on the edge of, or outside, towns, Blondel envisaged them as arcaded cloisters surrounded by the cenotaphs of those who had served their country. In the centre would be a great rusticated pyramid containing a sepulchral chapel in which the office of the dead would be continually celebrated. Cypresses and sepulchral urns would help create 'a somber tint which would contribute in no small way to giving the ensemble a lugubrious air calculated to impress at once on the eye that this was the home of shadows'.[13] Such imagery lay behind the pyramid-flanked mausoleum for James King with which Soane began his career as a student at the Royal Academy.

Sir William Chambers, Blondel's pupil and Soane's master, went so far as to envisage the

whole kingdom transformed into one magnificent vast Garden ... [which] might be rendered more splendid, if instead of disfiguring ... churches with monuments, [the] Chinese manner of erecting mausoleums by the sides of the roads was introduced ... and if all ... public bridges were adorned with triumphal arches, rostral pillars, bas-reliefs, statues, and other indications of victory, and glorious achievements in war; an empire transformed into a splendid Garden.[14]

Soane's future amanuensis Joseph Michael Gandy (1771–1843), as a student in Rome in 1794–7, wrote to his father about his ambition for creating an avenue of sepulchral monuments as a British Via Appia in either Hyde Park or Clapham Common. He believed that the need 'to raise such trophies to past eminent men' should be the subject of debate in Parliament.[15] In the meantime Jean-Louis Desprez had produced a design, dedicated to Voltaire, for a large cemetery for a Parisian parish which won him a *Prix d'émulation* in the Académie Royale d'Architecture in June 1766.[16] The central chapel, with a pyramidal form clearly indebted to Blondel, was set in a vast cloister inspired by the celebrated thirteenth-century Campo Santo in Pisa.[17] Soane owned a dramatic watercolour by Desprez of Somerset House,[18] while he had a large and handsome drawing of the Campo Santo at Pisa (fig. 3) prepared for his lectures on architecture delivered at the Royal Academy.[19]

Quatremère de Quincy wrote a long article under 'Cemetery' in the *Encyclopédie Méthodique* (1788), a work owned by Soane who also studied Quatremère's *De l'architecture égyptienne* in great detail. Following Blondel, Quatremère pointed to the Campo Santo at Pisa as a model for the modern cemetery, and also referred to the ancient Roman 'funerary cities' at Pozzuoli and Arles which had both been described as Elysian Fields. For Quatremère, the Campo Santo at Pisa was a speaking museum formed from frescoes, antique tombs, modern mausolea, inscriptions, and effigies of great men honoured by the republic of Pisa. Quatremère suggested that such places should be planted with cypresses and yews, dark brown foliage especially heightening the atmosphere of 'sacred melancholy'.

Quatremère's introduction of such themes was related to his response to the eighteenth-century tradition of romantic landscape gardening. From the early part of the century, funerary art invaded the garden and the stage, while the mood of stoical resignation in the face of death was soon transferred to poetry in popular works such as Edward Young's *Night Thoughts* (1742–5),[20] Robert Blair's *The Grave* (1743), and Gray's *Elegy* (1751). At Castle Howard and Stowe, three types of monument appeared: the 'Roman' tomb, evoking the idealised classical landscape of Claude or Poussin; the monument, such as a pyramid, commemorating someone buried elsewhere; and the tomb or mausoleum which formed an actual burial place.[21] Aware of its significance as the first monumental, free-standing tomb since antiquity,[22] Soane illustrated Hawksmoor's mausoleum at Castle Howard in his lectures (III.1). He also illustrated Chambers' monumental neo-antique mausoleum of 1751 for Frederick, Prince of Wales. This was designed, unusually, for a landscape setting, the royal gardens at Kew.

Quatremère de Quincy derived much of his information about the associational qualities of English garden design from a key work by Christian Hirschfeld, *Théorie de l'art des jardins* (5 vols., Leipzig 1779–85), the first three volumes of

Fig. 3 Soane, lecture illustration, *Campo Santo, Pisa* (SM)

which Soane owned. In the third volume, Hirschfeld praised the Elysian Fields at Stowe as the first example of the consecration of a whole area in a garden to the memory of the illustrious dead. Ever alive to the affective and moral associations of symbolical gardens, Hirschfeld recommended that the Stowe idea should be transferred to the creation of public cemeteries in the form of gardens.

Hirschfeld was equally enthusiastic about the landscaped park at Ermenonville, near Paris, created by the Marquis de Girardin. This contained an important area designed as an intimate Elysée for Girardin's friend, Rousseau, inspired by that in Rousseau's novel, *La Nouvelle Héloise* (1761). Following Rousseau's death at Ermenonville in 1778, he was buried on an island in the lake at Ermenonville, thus becoming the first person to be given a public burial in a garden. Soane, who was an avid reader of Rousseau, identifying with him emotionally as the supposed victim of organised persecution, was fully aware of the significance and emotional appeal of his tomb. Thus, in the frontispiece of one of his copies of Rousseau's *Confessions*, Soane made a quick ink sketch of Rousseau's tomb on the Ile des Peupliers at Ermenonville (I.4).

On his visit to Paris in 1819 with his pupil Henry Parke, Soane commissioned large and impressive watercolours from Parke of recent buildings for use as lecture illustrations. These included a distant view of Ledoux's *Barrière de la Villette*,[23] one of the most imposing of the 62 customs houses with which the officers of the Ferme Générale had encircled Paris from 1785. On being shown Ledoux's preliminary designs for the *barrières* on his visit to Paris in 1784, William Beckford had observed perceptively that, 'from their massive, sepulchral character [they] look more like the entrances of a Necropolis, a city of the dead, than of a city so damnably alive as this confounded capital'.[24]

In fact, the Elysian necropolis or garden cemetery, as presaged by the Marquis de Girardin at Ermenonville, by Ledoux in the *barrières*, and as recommended by Hirschfeld and Quatremère de Quincy, was to be first fully realised in the cemetery of Père Lachaise in Paris, initiated in 1804 by Napoleon as First Consul. Soane seems to have visited this remarkable cemetery in 1819, commis-

14

sioning impressive watercolours of it from Henry Parke (III.6,7).[25] In his fourth lecture at the Royal Academy, delivered at various points between 1810 and 1819, Soane admired the similar burial fields of the Ancients. He suggested that, rich with tombs and mausolea 'in honour of the dead [which] inspire the soul', they both recall and 'prepare the mind for those grand effects produced by the steeples, towers, spires, and domes of great cities, when viewed at a distance'. He was so far moved as to proclaim, 'Would to God this practice of placing tombs and sepulchral buildings on the sides of our public roads existed amongst us instead of our hiding them as we do in Westminster Abbey'.[26]

Soane's Designs for Mausolea and Monuments

Soane's life and career were constantly interwoven with the theme of death from at least the age of 22 when he designed a mausoleum to the memory of James King (XVIIa), a friend recently drowned on an outing that Soane had decided not to attend. His always introspective and frequently gloomy cast of mind doubtless meant that his feelings of relief were mingled with those of guilt when his *Triumphal Bridge* was awarded the Gold Medal later that year. His design for a mausoleum for James King can thus be interpreted as in part an act of reparation. Its cruciform plan was doubtless inspired by that of Peyre's *académie* design, published in his *Oeuvres d'architecture* in 1765, that key statement of the new Franco-Italian classicism. On this geometrically-planned base, Soane raised a massive structure boasting heavy rustication and pyramidal pavilions. This, as we have noted, was similar to the type of mausoleum recommended by Blondel, but its central domed rotunda was probably indebted to the design by Blondel's pupil, Chambers, for the mausoleum for Frederick, Prince of Wales. This is doubly likely in view of the fact that Chambers was Soane's own master at the Royal Academy schools.

The general air of magnificence and the rich

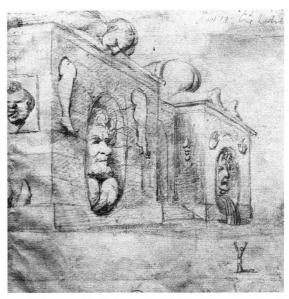

Fig. 4 Flaxman, *For the Exhibition of 1777, a Mausoleum adorn'd with Colossal Sculpture being an attempt at something in a New style* (detail) (Victoria and Albert Museum)

narrative ornament of Soane's mausoleum, including sarcophagi, urns, and mourning angels, were in harmony with the precepts of Thomas Sandby, Professor of Architecture at the Royal Academy, whose lectures Soane attended. John Flaxman parodied Soane's emphatic sculptural ornament in a sketch entitled, *For the Exhibition of 1777, a Mausoleum adorn'd with Colossal Sculpture being an attempt at something in a New style* (fig. 4).[27] Flaxman's building, an attempt at *architecture parlante*, was studded with carvings of human limbs and faces with bizarre expressions.

Nonetheless, Soane thought sufficiently highly of his ambitious King mausoleum to publish it in 1778 in his first book, *Designs in Architecture*, a collection of largely Chambersian designs for garden buildings. In the same year, when in Rome as a Gold Medallist, Soane heard the news of the death of William Pitt, Earl of Chatham, on 11 May 1778. Rather as Chambers, hearing in Rome of the death of Frederick, Prince of Wales, had designed a mausoleum for him, so Soane now designed a monumental mausoleum for the Earl of Chatham. He was doubtless prompted to make this by the enthusiasm for the Earl of his patron, the Bishop of Derry, and the arrival in Rome in 1778 of Chatham's nephew, Thomas Pitt, who became a friend of Soane.

Soane's Chatham mausoleum was a more austere version of his King mausoleum, though he exploited the traditional associations of Doric with manly vigour by replacing the Roman Doric with the baseless, fluted Greek Doric, perhaps in allusion to Chatham's stoic death. The plan has a somewhat phallic form, anticipating that of Ledoux's Oikéma,[28] but probably inspired by the similar disposition adopted by Piranesi in his reconstruction of the monumental tomb of Augustus in the Campus Martius in Rome.[29] Soane also adopted an unorthodox blend of Greek Doric columns with a sumptuous Corinthian frieze, incorporating the swags and bucrania of the Temple of Vesta at Tivoli. This deliberate bending of the supposed rules of the orders was doubtless an expression of the liberty which Soane believed had been allowed to the designers of mausolea in the ancient world. Wyatt was later to adopt the same conjunction of Doric columns and a frieze of swags and bucrania for his celebrated mausoleum at Brocklesby Park, Lincolnshire.

In keeping with what was to become his customary technique of repeating or reworking his own designs, Soane exhibited a version of his Chatham mausoleum, though omitting the reference to Chatham, at the Royal Academy in 1781. It reappeared once more in his *Sketches in Architecture* (1793), though now transmogrified into a 'National Mausoleum', not only for Chatham but 'for all the other great and virtuous characters who have deserved well of their country'.[30] Its role as an example of speaking architecture was underlined by the sarcophagi on the steps to the catacombs with inscriptions, 'attracting the attention of contemplative minds, furnishing them with ample scope for reflection, and preserving the memory of renowned persons'. The principal interiors would be 'decorated with bassi-relievi, statues, busts, historical paintings'. Here is the origin of what was to be a principal concern of Soane as the Napoleonic Wars unfolded: the ade-

quate commemoration in tombs and monuments of British naval and military heroes.

The first opportunities Soane had for erecting monuments were modest, yet even in these he gave careful consideration to finding appropriate form and symbolic ornament. He was keenly aware that free-standing columns in antiquity served as commemorative monuments, noting that Ulysses himself, according to Homer, raised a column on a hillock in memory of Elphenor, who broke his neck by falling over a staircase in the Palace of Circe.[31] Soane recorded that Pompey erected trophies and triumphal columns, and particularly stressed Trajan's Column in Rome which actually contained the emperor's ashes.

At Felbridge, Surrey, a tall Roman Doric column was raised from Soane's designs in 1785–6 to the memory of James Evelyn's parents (V).[32] Surmounted by a spirally-fluted urn, this featured a snake carved round the base. Soane chose this form because in ancient Egypt a snake in the form of a circle, with its tail in its mouth, was a symbol of eternity. Soane came to regret that he had designed Felbridge column at a point in his career before he had begun to pay proper attention to 'first principles'. By this he meant that he had acted illogically in raising an architrave, frieze, and cornice over the column, because such elements were essentially part of the horizontal entablature which connected a row of columns. In the meantime, however, he had built a similar memorial column for Philip Hills at Colne Park, Essex, 1790 (VII). This was of the Ionic order, bearing entwined snakes and a pineapple, also a symbol of eternity.

Amongst the many books Soane studied for the information they provided on the symbolism of classical ornament were *Recherches sur l'origine, l'esprit et les progrès des arts de la Grèce* (3 vols., London 1785), by the eccentric Pierre-François Hugues, self-styled Baron d'Hancarville, and the less recondite *L'Antiquité expliquée et représentée en figures* (10 vols. in 15, Paris 1719–24), by the Benedictine monk, Bernard de Montfaucon (1653–1741). In Volume V of his monumental

16

pictorial encylopaedic work, the most complete survey of Greek and Roman antiquities published up to that date, Montfaucon had included an illustrated survey of ancient tombs, mausolea, funerary monuments, and cinerary urns. Whereas previous artists and architects such as Robert Adam had raided Montfaucon for visual sources, Soane annotated the majority of the plates in Volume V with often quite detailed comments on the numerous symbolical attributes of gods such as Bacchus and Apollo.

Even in designing the modest Simeon Monument in Reading, Berkshire, in 1804 (VIII), Soane gave tremendous consideration to symbolical ornament, thus producing an object resembling a funereal or commemorative obelisk rather than the lamp-post which its patron had commissioned.[33] The triangular monument, adorned with Egyptian frets, is surmounted by segmental pediments adorned with beribboned wreaths which have funereal associations. Soane seems to have borrowed the device from the lids of Roman cinerary urns, and used it again in the Bosanquet Monument of 1806 and the Pitt Cenotaph of 1818. The crowning feature of the Simeon Monument is a cylindrical, spirally-fluted cinerary urn, capped by a pineapple or pine-cone, both perhaps a reference to the death of Simeon's brother in 1782. The fasces carved on the base of the obelisk presumably refer to the authority of the corporation under whose auspices the monument was erected.

In designing the mausoleum at Charlotte Street, for Noel Desenfans, in 1807, Soane, as we have already noted, was doubtless aware that the ancient Romans believed that their ancestors had buried their dead in their town houses. In his first sketches for extensions to his house at 12 Lincoln's Inn Fields in 1808, he denoted the basement portion as 'catacombs' with, on the south, a chamber marked 'mausoleum'. He may have intended this as a future resting place for himself, but the commission for a mausoleum from Sir Francis Bourgeois undoubtedly provided him with an opportunity to follow the earliest Roman practice of domestic sepulture. Moreover, the commission would enable him to put into practice the advice he had learned from Blondel and Le Camus de Mézières about the use of concealed light to create an atmosphere that was appropriately *'mystérieux et triste'*. Soane provided Bourgeois with a circular domed temple, dramatically top-lit and lined with Greek Doric columns, which was cut away on one side so as to provide a view through an arch into the smaller mausoleum itself.

When designing the Dulwich College mausoleum from 1811 to 1813, Soane closely followed the form of his first mausoleum for Bourgeois, but was able to create an impressive exterior echoing Roman tombs on the Via Appia. The building was possibly also indebted to Robert Adam's towers at Mistley church, Essex. It contained no Christian symbols, though snakes featured prominently in the spandrels.

Work on Dulwich was completed in 1814. In the following year, Soane's melancholy 'Etruscan' temperament found its fullest expression in the total gloom into which he was cast by the death of his wife in November. His despair was heightened by his belief that her death had been hastened, if not actually caused, by the shock she sustained on reading the vicious attack on Soane's work written by their son, George, in *The Champion* newspaper in September 1815 (see I.5).

There can be little doubt that Soane's despondency was near suicidal. He was much struck by the suicide of the distinguished lawyer Sir Samuel Romilly following the death of his own wife in November 1818. Making notes in that month from Rousseau, with whom he always identified emotionally, Soane wrote of Romilly, himself an early follower of Rousseau,

"A want of rest, and a perpetual contemplation of the death of his wife had disturbed the whole order of the nerves. They were in a state of the most painful excitement". Good God is not this my case? and yet I have borne up against this very feeling for more than three years! but –.[36]

We know from Soane's notes on his reading of Winckelmann that he regarded himself as a latter-day Etruscan, sunk in the reflective melancholy of a nation of tomb-builders. Winckelmann claimed that we could tell from the 'religious services and customs' of the Etruscans that they had a 'more bilious and melancholic temperament than the Greeks'. Winckelmann also noted that, according to Aristotle, this temperament was usually the lot of the greatest men because it was 'fitted to profound investigation'. But he also pointed out that 'it gives rise to emotions of too violent a nature, and the senses are not affected with that gentle agitation which renders the soul perfectly susceptible to beauty'. Soane underlined the whole of this passage, adding in the margin, 'I believe this is very true'.[35]

Following his wife's interment on 1 December 1815 in the burial ground of St Giles-in-the-Fields, adjoining Old St Pancras church, Soane threw himself into the task of designing a monument to mark her tomb. By February 1816 he had settled on the final form which is that of a convex domed canopy, supported on four square piers, all in Portland stone, sheltering a monument in a rarer material, white marble. The inner monument or sarcophagus is itself in the form of a canopy, though carried in this case by four Ionic columns. Sir John Summerson has beautifully analysed the great variety of 'memory-threads woven into this monument', ranging from a prehistoric dolmen to a rectangular Roman tomb illustrated in Montfaucon's *Antiquité expliquée*,[36] and including the by now familiar pineapple and self-devouring snake. Summerson has also convincingly suggested that the form of the outer canopy and the space it shelters 'can be interpreted as the breakfast-room at 13 Lincoln's Fields turned inside out, the domical surface of the room's ceiling being externalized'.[37] Such an interpretation emphasises the ubiquitous presence of the tomb or sarcophagus as a constant form-giver in Soane's work. For example, his domed clock by Vulliamy, still in the Breakfast Room, is designed on the same principal as the Soane Tomb.

In the open screen dividing the Dining Room from the Library at 13 Lincoln's Inn Fields, Soane incorporated a painted wood model of the Soane Tomb enclosed in a brass-framed glass case: a gloomy souvenir to accompany the activities of dining or reading. Doubtless made in 1816, it survives today in the same position, bearing on the dome the melancholy inscription, *'Chère amie je ne peux plus entendre ta voix – apprends mois ce que je dois faire – pour remplir tes souhaits'*. The design of the monument was also coloured by Soane's understanding that he was creating a monument to himself as well as to his wife. In March 1816 he wrote to his old friend Rowland Burdon of Castle Eden, with whom he had visited the Greek temple at Segesta, to ask for advice on a suitable inscription for the tomb.[38] His own proposal was the lines from Virgil, '*His saltem accumulem donis et fungar inani munere*' ('Let me, at all events, pile up these funeral rites and perform vain offices').[39] The sense of hopelessness and negativity conveyed by this choice of inscription suggests that his obsession with the tombs of the pagan world had led him far from the world of Christian hope. In 1823, he suffered the pain of seeing his eldest son, John, buried in the tomb in St Pancras Gardens, while he was himself buried there on 30 January 1837.

In the meantime Soane was invited to design a memorial monument of a different kind, the so-called Pitt Cenotaph at the National Debt Redemption Office in Old Jewry.[40] In the unusual building erected from Soane's designs in 1818–19, a life-size bronze statue by Sir Richard Westmacott of Pitt,[41] enthroned and robed, sat beneath a lofty domed space of which the first floor was surrounded by a circular peristyle of Corinthian columns, chosen in accordance with Soane's belief that, 'Art cannot go beyond the Corinthian order'.[42] This grandiose, if theatrical, space recalled the dramatically-lit inner halls or 'tribunes' which Soane had designed for Tyringham and Wotton. He called it a cenotaph in recognition of the fact that it did not contain the actual corpse of Pitt, though his fondness for the paraphernalia of death led him in an early design to include cinerary urns on shelves in the side recesses.

The Belzoni Sarcophagus and the Monk's Tomb

Five years after the completion of the National Debt Redemption Office, Soane acquired what was the most expensive and, in some ways, prestigious, object of his entire collection, the sarcophagus, or outmost container of the coffin, of Pharaoh Seti I of the XIXth Dynasty (c.1300 BC).[43] Discovered by the Italian Egyptologist Giovanni Battista Belzoni in Seti's tomb in the Valley of the Kings in 1817, it was deposited in the British Museum in 1821 in the expectation that it would be purchased by the Trustees. When they found the asking price of £2,000 excessive, Soane was delighted to step in with an offer of exactly that sum. When the massive object of oriental alabaster, nine and a half feet long, arrived in May 1824, a section of the wall at the rear of 13 Lincoln's Inn Fields was removed to receive it. It was then lowered by ropes through the floor of the Dome to its resting place in the crypt, an area which, as we have seen, Soane had intended as early as 1808 to serve as mausoleum and catacomb. Just a few days before its arrival, news reached London of Belzoni's death in Africa. As a result, Soane referred to it as 'the Belzoni sarcophagus', thus somehow adding to its historic resonances the role of shrine to its modern discoverer.

In March 1825 he gave a series of three evening receptions at which over 890 guests were invited to view 'The Belzoni Sarcophagus and other antiquities ... by lamp light'. The outside of the house was impressively illuminated with 256 lamps in glass containers, while more mysterious and dramatic effects were achieved within, where the basement area and ground floors were subtly lit with oil lamps and candles, chandeliers and candelabra hired at great expense from William Collins the stained-glass manufacturer. Helen Dorey has recently analysed the surviving bills, thus enabling

us to reconstruct the varied impressions made, for example, by the three lamps placed outside the dining room window in the Monument Court, or by the presence in the Picture Room of a chandelier, four lamps and 'a large looking glass', all hired from Collins. To provide the mysterious contrast between light and dark envisaged at Dulwich, the basement at the Soane Museum contained much less illumination than the upper floors (fig. 5). In the generally darkened basement, the Belzoni sarcophagus was picked out with the illumination provided by 'one two-light pedestal lamp, one single-light pedestal lamp with reflector and seven "japanned lamps"'.[44]

It is likely that Soane placed lamps inside the sarcophagus since it was noted for its translucency. If so, the whole scene, as Summerson noted, echoed the evocative drawing by Gandy, *The Tomb of Merlin* (1815), which Gandy had offered to Soane in 1816 'as a mark of my esteem and gratitude'.[45] Here, Gandy had depicted a mysterious, vaulted crypt housing an exotic, centrally-placed shrine glowing translucently so as to constitute the principal source of light in the whole interior.[48] The analogy with Gandy is underlined by the following passage by Barbara Hofland in Soane's *Description of the House and Museum on the North Side of Lincoln's Inn Fields* (1835–6). In her romantic account of the Belzoni sarcophagus 'viewed by lamplight', she wrote how,

> Seen by this medium every surrounding object ... becomes subservient to the sarcophagus ... and all else are but accessories to its dignity and grandeur ... sweet and tender memories unite us to the grave.
>
> Deep masses of shadow, faint gleams that rise like *ignes fatui* from the adjoining crypt, lights that shine like lustrous halos round marble heads ... as in a dream of the poets' elysium. ...figure after figure emerges from the crypt and corridors, where they had loitered in the gloom: they assemble round the sarcophagus, which sheds from within a pale, unearthly light... Pensive is every countenance, and soft is every falling foot-

Fig. 5 Soane, *The Dome Looking East* (SM)

step; yet in gentle accents many a voice breathes thanks to him who hath rolled back the current of time to shew them glorious visions of the past, yet taught them to feel, even in the hour of pleasure itself, that, "The paths of glory lead but to the grave".[47]

Here, I believe is the authentic voice of Soane. A close friend of Mrs Hofland, he commissioned her to make significant additions to the text of his *Description*, aware that his pen did not rise to expressing the emotions and effects he wished his work to convey. This is scarcely surprising since his architecture speaks sufficiently eloquently on its own. Indeed, as Lukacher has observed, the Soane Museum is so full of 'creative gestures of self-interment' that the voice of Soane can be heard from beyond the grave: thus here, as at Dulwich, we are 'all but treated to utterances from the spirit world'.[48]

In studying Quatremère de Quincy's *De l'architecture égyptienne* (1803), Soane had been impressed by the claim that Egyptian architecture had been a kind of symbolic language. Always anxious to give his own architecture an appropriate character or meaning, he was struck by the importance of the Belzoni sarcophagus as, in his words, a 'marvellous effort of human industry and perseverance ... supposed to be at least three thousand years old ... [and] illustrative of the customs, arts, religion and government of a very ancient and learned people'. He explained that it 'is covered externally and internally with hieroglyphics, comprehending a written language which it is to be hoped the labours of modern literati will render intelligible'. He would doubtless have been intensely gratified to discover that the texts are from *The Book of the Dead*, while most of the figures, scenes, and hieroglyphics relate to *The Book of the Gates (or Pylons)*, a guide to the Underworld through which the souls of worshippers of Osiris and Ra would pass after death.

Soane's house-cum-museum was shortly to contain yet another tomb, that of the 'monk' supposedly buried below the window of the 'Monk's Parlour', or 'Parloir of Padre Giovanni'. This formed part of the area which Soane created in 1824 in the yard and basement at the back of 14 Lincoln's Inn Fields. Occupying the space below his new Picture Gallery of 1824, the low and dark 'Monk's Parlour' looked through a window into the 'Monk's Yard'. This yard, at the rear of 14 contained a couple of medieval Gothic arches which, having been salvaged by Soane from Westminster, he called the monk's 'cloister'. It is hard to enter into the mind of the Soane who created this half-mocking, half-serious, fantasy home for a deceased monk, Padre Giovanni (Father John), who was obviously partly intended as a self-portrait. He claimed that, 'The interest created in the mind of the spectator, on visiting the abode of the monk, will not be weakened by wandering among the ruins of his once noble monastery'. These cramped dark spaces, full of the souvenirs of a despoiled medieval past, were thus intended to move the mind to the same reflections on the decay of civilisation and the vanity of human wishes as were the grander remains of the superior classical culture in other parts of his house. Death, as always, was at the core of his emotional range: he thus added that, 'The Tomb of the monk adds to the gloomy scenery of this hallowed place'.

Soane went so far as to hang a skeleton in the Monk's Cell. This had come from the studio of his friend John Flaxman whose widow gave it to Soane some time during the last six months of his life.[49] There are further skeletons, miniature ones, in the crypt at 13 Lincoln's Inn Fields. These are housed in four cork models of 'Etruscan' tombs where they are surrounded by what Soane called 'a variety of Etruscan vases and implements of sacrifice'.[50] Soane originally displayed these on the ground floor but moved them down to the Crypt in the gloomy basement where their macabre qualities blended with the Belzoni sarcophagus, a carved wooden lid from an Egyptian mummy-case of about 1250 BC, and other souvenirs of death. The area of the Crypt known as the Catacombs was originally lined with three tiers of box-like recesses containing cinerary urns, top-lit through an opening in the ceiling.[51] The effect was thus close to that of the tombs and ruins of ancient Rome, for example the 'Sepulchral Vault in the Vigna Casali on the right of the Via Appia', as seductively depicted in a book of twelve engravings owned by Soane, *Via Appia illustrata ab urbe Roma ad Capuam* (Rome, 1794).

Soane and the Ruin

The future of the Soane Museum as a ruin was envisaged by Soane in a remarkable document of 1812, *Crude Hints towards an History of my House in L[incoln's] I[nn] Fields*.[52] Here, even while he was in the process of building the house, he imagined it as a ruin, inspected by visitors speculating on its original purpose and form. Puzzled by 'the ruins and very extensive assemblage of fragments of ancient works partially buried and in some degree attached to a building in this metropolis of an apparently late date', they might suppose the place to be an architectural museum, 'a Heathen Temple to Vesta, or the palace of an Enchanter or a Convent for Nuns'.[53]

Soane's preoccupation with death and decay found a natural focus in the ruin. Here he was in harmony with his visionary disciple, Joseph Gandy, whom we already seen visiting the tombs along the Via Appia and envisaging their recreation in a London park. In 1795 Gandy entered the Concorso Clementino of the Accademia di San Luca in Rome with a design for a *Sepulchral Chapel in a Circular Piazza*, which was the subject set for the first class in architecture that year.[54] From this point on, the drama of sepulture was to be a constant theme in Gandy's work. It can be said to have been present even earlier, for in 1786 he was a pupil in the office of James Wyatt who was then at work on one of the most striking of all English neoclassical mausolea, that at Brocklesby Park, Lincolnshire (fig. 6). Built for Lord Yarborough, Wyatt's handsome rotunda with its Doric peristyle was shown to the public as a popular spectacle, complete with Visitors' Book. Elements of Brocklesby were to feature in Gandy's sepulchral chapel for the Concorso Clementino. Soane was also familiar with the Brocklesby mausoleum, for Turner sent him a print of its interior in 1804.[55] This had been engraved after a watercolour which Lord Yarborough had commissioned from Turner in 1797. Another view of the interior[56] featured in Turner's lectures on perspective at the Royal Academy as an example of coloured light filtering through stained glass.[57]

Back in England, Gandy exhibited drawings at the Royal Academy such as *Sepulchral Chamber* in 1800, and the even more spectacular *Design for a Cenotaph* in 1804, which was bought by Thomas

Fig. 6 The Mausoleum at Brocklesby Park, Lincs.

perspective, cut-away to reveal the methods of construction, curiously resembles a vast ruined building such as the Forum Romanum or Baths of Diocletian which had been partially excavated. Referring in his Royal Academy lectures to the mausolea of Hadrian and of Cecilia Metella, Soane observed that,

> Works that might have defied the efforts of time are now with their battlements and embrasures, become mere monuments of the insufficiency of our endeavours, and of the mutability of all human expectations.

He went on to claim that, 'ruins may be considered as histories open to all the world'. Such a belief lies behind Gandy's remarkable painting of 1832, *Architectural ruins – a vision* (fig. 8). Here, Soane's Rotunda and adjacent Consols Office at the Bank of England are shown in Piranesian decay as a commentary on the vanity of human wishes. In exhibiting this picture, Soane underlined the point by adding to it Prospero's words from *The Tempest*, *'The cloud-capt towers, the gorgeous palaces, / The solemn temples, the great globe itself, / Yea, all which it inherit shall dissolve'*.

Monuments for Heroes

Finally, we should note that the eighteenth-century belief that civic virtue should be expressed in the erection of public monuments was given enormous new impetus by the Revolutionary and Napoleonic Wars with the resultant need to erect monuments to military heroes, living and dead.[60] It was in this world that Soane's belief in both civic virtue and in tombs and mausolea was to find appropriate expression.[61] Apart from his own family tomb in St Giles' burial ground, none of the few monuments and memorials he designed for private patrons were of much consequence. However, a new phase in British sculpture was opened in 1795 when Parliament voted money for the erection of public monuments in St Paul's Cathedral to national heroes who had died in the

Hope for display in his house-cum-museum in Duchess Street. It is, of course, to Gandy that we owe the most brilliant and evocative of all images of Soane's interiors, beginning with his Breakfast Room and Library at Pitzhanger Manor of 1800, designed in the form of Roman tomb chambers. Eerie, moonlit, and frequently funereal in tone, Gandy's illustrations culminate in his late and compellingly intense depiction of 1832 of Soane's Freemasons' Council Chamber (1828), entitled *Interior of the edifice devoted exclusively to Freemasonry ... an evening view made after the completion of the building*.[58] As Lukacher entertainingly observes of this room, 'Imagine a high Regency funeral parlor crossed with a lavishly-appointed dungeon from a Gothic novel, and this might well be the result'.[59]

Gandy's *Bird's-eye view of the Bank of England* (1830) (fig. 7), though nominally an aerial

Fig. 7 Gandy, *Bird's-eye view of the Bank of England* (SM)

Fig. 8 Gandy, *Architectural ruins – a vision* (SM)

23

war against France. The foundations for such a scheme had been laid by Sir Joshua Reynolds who, attempting to secure public commissions for members of the Royal Academy in 1773, had proposed adorning St Paul's Cathedral with, as he put it, 'monuments of famous men ... and ... history paintings'.[62] Soane, as Professor of Architecture at the Royal Academy from 1806, fully shared these ambitions, as did his friend and colleague, John Flaxman, appointed first Professor of Sculpture at the Royal Academy in 1810. Indeed, in his opening lecture, Flaxman claimed that the creation of this chair was in consequence of the recent provision of monuments to British heroes and patriots.[63]

Competitions for military and naval monuments were announced in 1799 and 1807. The first, following the Battle of the Nile in 1798, was managed by a Committee for raising a Naval Pillar or Monument. Both Soane and Flaxman responded, the former with a design for a National Mausoleum which he exhibited at the Royal Academy in 1799, and the latter with a project for a monumental *Britannia Triumphans* at Greenwich. After the Battle of Waterloo in 1815, the project was revived. Thus Soane exhibited designs for a monument at the Royal Academy in 1816 and 1818. In 1828 he made a design in response to the decision to raise a public monument to Frederick Augustus, Duke of York and Albany. (XVIIe) Soane's design took the form of a Sepulchral Church and Military Chapel, based on his unexecuted project of 1800 for a triangular Greek Doric church at Tyringham. In July 1829 he was one of nine architects invited to enter the limited competition for the Duke of York's monument which the committee had by now recommended should take the form of a triumphal column, similar to that of Trajan in Rome.[64] Nonetheless, Soane's design for the monument, submitted to the committee on 7 August 1829, still took the form of a domed Sepulchral Church or monopteral temple, containing a statue of the Duke of York. He described it as a 'superb Sepulchral Church, with lofty Catacombs ... for ... the reception of the Remains of those Heroes who had fought in defence of their Country'.[65]

Standing in St James's Park, facing Horse Guards Parade and opposite Waterloo Place, Soane's monument was to be a prominent feature of the processional way which he proposed for the ceremonial heart of London. Its exterior was richly adorned with Greek Doric columns, sarcophagi, lions, and caryatids, while there were more caryatids inside, facing each other in pairs, as well as numerous busts crowned with the wreaths of heroes. As a striking gesture of his belief in the importance of a monument to the Duke of York, he contributed the large sum of £1,000 to help defray the cost of the colossal statue in August 1829. Finally, in 1831 he prepared an ambitious design for a Wellington monument on which he was still at work in December 1836, the month before he died.

FOOTNOTES

1 From a description of the Belzoni Sarcophagus contributed by Barbara Hofland to Soane, 1835–6, p. 39
2 Colvin, 1991, p. 333
3 See Watkin, 1996
4 Lubersac, 1775
5 Patte, 1765
6 First published in the *Architectural Review*, March 1978, reprinted in Summerson, 1990, pp. 121–42
7 Horace, *Ars poetica*, 105–6
8 Boffrand, 1745, p. 27. My translation
9 Nicolas Le Camus de Mézières, *Le génie de l'architecture; ou, l'analogie de cet art avec nos sensations*, Paris 1780
10 Sir John Soane's Museum (hereafter SM) Soane Case 160
11 SM Drawer 20/4/4, based on Giovanni Battista Piranesi, *Le Antichità Romane*, Rome 1756, III, 2nd frontispiece
12 Laugier, 1765, p. 240
13 Blondel, II, 1771, p. 341. My translation
14 Chambers, 1772, pp. 133–4
15 Lukacher, 1987; Arbor 1983, p. 8
16 Montclos, 1984, pp. 83–5

17 Etlin, 1984, pp. 49–50

18 He bought the Desprez drawings at the sale of Chambers' prints and drawings in 1811 (Harris, 1970, pp. 185–6 & pl. 165)

19 SM, Drawer 76/7/5

20 See Curl, 1994, pp. 92–118

21 See Colvin, 1991, pp. 328–9

22 See Curl, 1980, p. 179

23 SM Drawer 22/8/6

24 William Beckford to the Hon. Louisa Beckford (John Walter Oliver, *The Life of William Beckford*, Oxford 1932, pp. 172–3)

25 SM Drawer 22/6/1–3

26 Bolton, ed., 1929, p. 72. Quoting from this passage in *Soane and After*, 1987, p. 59, Giles Waterfield pointed out that C.H. Tatham had followed this precept by placing his mausoleum at Trentham, Staffordshire (1807–8), directly on the public road

27 See also Ruffinière du Prey, 1982, fig. 4.12

28 Claude-Nicolas Ledoux, *Architecture considérée sous le rapport de l'art, des moeurs, et de la législation*, Paris, 1804, pl. 104, a book Soane owned and on which he made notes

29 Giovanni Battista Piranesi, *Il Campo Marzio dell'antica Roma*, Rome 1762, pl. IX

30 Soane, 1793, p. iv

31 Bolton, ed., 1929, p. 59

32 In 1928 the column was moved to Lemmington Hall, Northumberland

33 See Windsor, 1993, pp. 271–82

34 SM, Soane Case 164, f. [179]

35 Winckelmann, 1784 (SM AL 36H)

36 Montfaucon, 1719, V, part 1, pl. CXXII

37 Summerson, *op. cit.*, pp. 135–6

38 See Rowland Burdon to Soane, 27 March 1816 (SM Private Archives)

39 The actual translation of the *Aeneid*, vi, 885, in Soane's copy of *The Works of Virgil in Latin and English*, London 1753, III, p. 269, in which he ticked the relevant passage in Latin, reads, more succinctly, 'These gifts at least, these honours I'll bestow'

40 Soane's building was demolished in 1900 and the statue of Pitt subsequently bought by Pembroke College, Cambridge, Pitt's old college, where it stands today outside the Library

41 See Busco, 1994, pp. 74–5

42 Bolton, 1929, p. 35

43 See Dorey, 1991, pp. 26–35

44 Dorey, 1991, p. 32

45 Joseph Gandy to Soane, 30 July 1816 (SM Private Correspondence). Soane did not accept the offer. The painting was acquired by his friend Sir Richard Westmacott and is today in the RIBA Drawings Collection

46 For a detailed analysis of this painting, see Lukacher, 1983

47 Soane, 1835, pp. 38–9

48 Lukacher, 1983, p. 45

49 Thornton and Dorey, 1992, p. 58 and fig. 54

50 Thornton and Dorey, p. 66 and fig. 64

51 This arrangement was altered when the Ante-Room on the ground floor was formed in 1889–90

52 SM AL Soane Case 31

53 Ibid, f. 43

54 Lukacher, 1987; Arbor 1983, pp. 6–24 & pls. 4–7

55 Bolton, ed., 1927, p. 112

56 Reproduced in Davies, 1992, fig. 13

57 See *Turner & Architecture*, Tate Gallery, London 1988, p. 14

58 See Watkin, 1995

59 Lukacher, 1987, p. 150

60 See Yarrington (1980), 1988

61 On the historical background, see Fehl, 1972

62 Cited from Whinney, 1988, p. 362

63 Flaxman, 1829, pp. 1–2 (SM AL 31A)

64 The other architects were Burn, Cockerell, Gandy Deering, Nash, Smirke, B.D. Wyatt, and Wyatville (Public Record Office, *Works* 20 5/1, committee minute 4 July 1829). See Yarrington (1980), 1988, p. 254

65 John Soane, *Designs for Public and Private Buildings*, 1828, p. 5

Fig. 1 Hugh Douglas Hamilton, *Portrait of Col. Richard Mansergh St George*, c. 1796 (National Gallery of Ireland, Dublin)

Roger Bowdler

Et in Arcadia Ego: The Neoclassical Tomb 1760–1840

Hugh Douglas Hamilton's portrait of Col. Richard St George Mansergh St George (fig. 1) epitomises the act of classical mourning. It was painted shortly after the death of his wife in 1795, and depicts the disconsolate cavalry officer standing beside a chaste raised sarcophagus, ringed by cypresses. St George's pained gaze, slumped stance and abandoned 'Tarleton' helmet lying amid foliage all speak of his desolation; her tomb is his support. Darkness was closing in on St George, who followed his wife to the grave in 1798. *Non immemor*, 'Forgotten not', reads the stern inscription. An icon of Rousseauesque sentiment, the portrait epitomises the place of the tomb as the focus of grief.

This essay looks at churchyard monuments, *other* than those by Soane, erected in the London area during his lifetime. These outdoor tombs have received considerably less attention than either interior funerary monuments[1] or mausolea,[2] and it is fully time that attention was paid to them before they all disintegrate into their constituent parts and are lost forever.

Monuments were the embodiments of memory. Although capable (like any other social convention) of insincerity,[3] they were more likely to be born out of deeply-felt sentiments. Few other artistic or architectural commissions could vie with tombs on this score. Just how much attention could be given to a sepulchre is demonstrated by the following example. Lord Dacre died in 1794 and was commemorated with 'a very handsome monument, composed of beautiful white marble, with a large urn encircled and the figure of a snake on top'. He had left the huge annual sum of £40 to be spent on the upkeep of the tomb in the churchyard of St Margaret's, Lee, near Lewisham.

It was initially washed every Saturday by a servant, to preserve its chaste splendour. 'Lady Dacre, during her widowhood of fourteen years, showed an extraordinary instance of conjugal love and affection by offering up a prayer in the churchyard alone, every evening during fair weather, until a highway robber demanded her gold watch and chain, which she very reluctantly gave him'.[4] Her devotions at her husband's tomb presented the quintessentially classical spectacle – familiar from countless mourning rings – of the mourning woman beside an urn in the sylvan setting of a leafy churchyard.

Countless neoclassical church monuments took tombs as their subject. Richard Solly's monument by John Bacon the younger, erected in Worcester Cathedral after his death in 1803, may stand for a legion of other memorials (fig. 2). It shows Mrs Solly and her three young children beside the casket of the *paterfamilias*: her grief is underscored by the insouciance of the infants, too young to know what the casket contains. If one considers what is depicted, one realises the growing prestige of the outdoor tomb: the return to antique models implied the return to antique modes of burial – if not cremation, at least an open-air tomb. The same act of grief and remembrance was performed around the scores of neoclassical tombs that survive in churchyard and cemetery alike. If we find their austere forms cold and unmoving, it is because the imagination needs to supply the scene with its long-vanished principal players: the mourners. It is this emotional piquancy that endows these tombs with an interest beyond the purely architectural. Their stony forms were once animated by a very human grief.

A rare instance of an outdoor tomb with

Fig. 2 John Bacon the younger: monument to Richard Solly (d. 1803), Worcester Cathedral

sculpted figures is to be found in Finchley church-yard, where the chest tomb of Elizabeth Norris (d.1779) is crowned with the reclining effigy of a cowled woman, Agrippina-like and life-size, contemplating a casket (fig. 3). Generally, however, Remembrance had to conjure up both the deceased and their attributes for itself. This was well expressed in a stanza written by Lady Saye and Sele on the death in childbirth of her daughter Maria, Countess von Gersdorff, in 1826, which adorned an urn-topped pedestal in her garden:

The glimmering twilight, and the doubtful dawn,
Shall see my steps, to this sad spot return;
Constant as crystal dews empart the lawn,
Shall my sad tears bedew Maria's urn.
Haply the muse, as with unceasing sighs
She keeps late vigils on the urn reclined,
May see light groups of pleasant visions rise,
Of phantoms glide, but of celestial kind.[5]

These phantoms, the elegy explains, consist of Simplicity, Candour, Innocence, Elegance and

28

Beauty, each of which bewailed the Countess's untimely death. Thus were the chill forms of the neoclassical tomb brought alive by the memory-conjured world of the spirit. Remembrance, and the tomb, perpetuated the place of the dead.

Tombs, since the Reformation, had been classical.[6] So potent was the allure of the antique tomb and so well-studied was the classical elegiac tradition that the Anglican had little difficulty in adopting heathen models for his memorials. Columns, obelisks, urns, sarcophagi, busts, stelae, statues, columbaria, mausolea: each manifestation of the funerary antique found its way into the monuments of the sixteenth and seventeenth centuries. What distinguished the neoclassical tomb from the classical one was purity.

Purity is the crucial concept in terms of classicism and neoclassicism. The return to correctness of scale and setting, prompted by archaeological inquiry, travel and the dissemination of clear and credible engravings of classical antiquities all facilitated the search for classical authenticity, a search which acquired increasing intensity in Soane's lifetime. Monuments were whitewashed, both to protect the stone (which in the London area was almost always Portland) from the elements but also to endow them with the brightness of Pentellic or Carrara marble. Marble was known to be unsuitable for outside employment in damp London churchyards: 'the white marble placed in the open air, would soon have been spoiled, and would not have answered the purpose of securing his respected remains', wrote Thomas Banks' daughter Lavinia in 1805 as she justified his simple tomb in Paddington churchyard, which consisted of a ledger upon brick courses.[7]

It is important, before considering the architectural or sculptural side of neoclassical tombs, to be aware of the setting of burials, and of how the status of outdoor burial in churchyard or cemetery came to be acceptable to all classes. Greek and Roman monuments,[8] in the main, were outdoor affairs. For this reason, the rise of external monuments of high status that can be discerned

Fig. 3 Detail of monument to Elizabeth Norris (d. 1779), churchyard of St Mary the Virgin, Finchley, London Borough of Barnet

in the later eighteenth century was one of the less noticed manifestations of neoclassicism. Like the Ancients before them, the later Georgians turned to extra-mural places of burial out of choice. This shift had been a long time coming. Evelyn, Wren, Hawksmoor and Vanbrugh had all expressed preferences for burial outside the walls of churches, and outside the walls of cities.[9] From the mid-eighteenth century onwards, an increasing number of impressive outdoor tombs began to be constructed which drew on classical precedent. It is with these tombs, rather than their lavish interior counterparts, that this essay is concerned.

Churchyard burial, in England at least, had long signified lowly status. Only a handful of medieval outdoor monuments of any pretensions can be found in English churchyards.[10] In 1726 a polemic by the Rev. Thomas Lewis entitled *Churches no Charnel House* was published, urging outdoor burial for all, but it does not appear to have met with marked success. One of the first Anglican cemeteries (as opposed to a churchyard) in England was the joint burial ground for the new churches of St George's, Bloomsbury and St George the Martyr, Holborn.[11] So reluctant were

Fig. 4 Headstone to Samuel Cock (d. 1726), churchyard of St Lawrence Whitchurch, Little Stanmore, London Borough of Harrow

persons to be buried in it – possibly because cemeteries were seen as the province of Jews, Quakers and other Dissenters – that the first person to be interred there, Robert Nelson, chose this location in order 'to overcome the aversion that has been discovered to its use'. Not surprisingly, outdoor monuments of high status tended to be exceptional up to the later eighteenth century. The grander monuments of the earlier part of the century tended to be put up by aspirant merchants, such as the queer triangular tomb of the 1740s in St Lawrence's churchyard, Morden, to the Mauvilains, a family of calico manufacturers of Huguenot descent in the Wandle Valley. By the end of the century, churchyard burial had lost some its stigma and in a churchyard like that of St Margaret's, Lee, the Dacre tomb could stand next

door to one commemorating a Lord Mayor of London, and another to a Cornish baronet and MP. Nowhere was the reaction against intramural burial more evident than in Kensal Green Cemetery, where two of George III's children, Augustus Frederick, Duke of Sussex (d.1843) and Princess Sophia (d.1848) were buried beneath tombs that were, respectively, massive and elegant.[12] This return to burial on the ancient model provided an immense encouragement to the erection of classically-inspired monuments. Soane was but the best-known designer of *all'antica* memorials at an exceptionally busy period of tomb-building.

Precious few churchyard memorials[13] remain in the London area from the seventeenth century that are still legible. Survivals are more numerous from around 1720 onwards and are more likely to be legible, but the toll taken by the elements and acid rain has been severe.

There were three main types of outdoor tomb around 1800: the headstone, the chest tomb or sarcophagus, and the pedestal monument, generally supporting an urn. In addition to these were rare mausolea, the occasional obelisk or pillar, and a few oddities that defy categorisation. By far the most common material in the London area was Portland stone; some chests were built out of brick, and a small but very significant number of exceptional tombs were built from London's only indigenous stone: the artificial Coade stone.[14] Next to nothing is now left of the more humble wooden graveboards and markers once common in this area; immortality through monuments was a commodity that could be purchased. A clear hierarchy operated: headstones were an artisanal type of memorial, as the frequent references to trades within their epitaphs make clear. Chest tombs were the preserve of the gentry and often sported armorial cartouches. This hierarchy remained in place until the later nineteenth century, when the monumental free-for-all of the commercial cemetery took over, although even in Soane's day the conventions that harnessed tomb design were slackening.

Neoclassicism had a fatal impact upon the most

Fig. 5 Monogrammist WF, *Churchyard of St Paul, Covent Garden*, c. 1809 (SM)

common monument, the headstone. The golden age of tombstones (in the London area at least) occurred in the first half of the eighteenth century. Richly scrolled surrounds, characterful reliefs of cherubs and skulls (the emblems of resurrection and decay, the twin faces of Christian death), varied lettering: these are encountered on hundreds of headstones and remain surprisingly unstudied.[15] That erected at St Lawrence Whitchurch, Little Stanmore, to Samuel Cock (d.1726) (fig. 4) is a good exemplar of the vigorously rustic brand of classicism that marks the best of the genre: its scrolls and fluted pilasters pay lip-service to the Antique, while its form and fielded panel, and the piratical skull and crossbone, owe much to the lingering tradition of Artisan Mannerism. From the 1770s onwards, silhouettes became less exuberant, the relief carving diminished in depth, and the symbolism shed its emphasis on mortality for a milder vocabulary of Christian mourning and consolation in which the cherub's head became ever more common. As

with grander monuments, plainness came to be seen as a virtue under the growing influence of the antique stele.

The impact this had on the churchyard can be judged in the watercolour of the west front of St Paul's, Covent Garden, with which Soane chose to illustrate the Tuscan order in his fourth Royal Academy lecture,[16] first delivered in 1809 (fig. 5). The severity of the 'handsomest barn in England' was offset by the densely thronged churchyard, in which the occasional older headstone is jostled by a phalanx of classical stones and chests, their severity of outline only mitigated by the occasional acroterion. Soane's use of chaste profiles, geometric austerity, of reserve and emptiness, did not emerge from a void. By the time his memorials had begun to be erected in the mid-1780s, such characteristics were informing the output of the humblest village mason as well as of the leading metropolitan designers.

The next most common memorial form, the tomb chest or sarcophagus, showed similar signs

31

of change. The literal meaning of the word *sarcophagus* is 'flesh eater': they were stone coffins in which corpses were placed and in which they decayed. It is important to remember that the sarcophagi in Anglican churchyards were for show only: they were constructed *over* the brick burial vaults in which the coffined corpses were placed.[17] Just as the corners of Wyatt's Darnley Mausoleum (III.2, 3) boast strigillated sarcophagi which were never intended to be filled, but were to be read as symbols of the building's function as repository for the dead, so innumerable sarcophagi and chests were constructed to mark a resting place of status, to provide a simulacrum of the actual receptacle of the body, and to echo antique models. The Soane family tomb was exceptional in the emphasis placed on the steps leading down into the vault.

The earliest neoclassical sarcophagi in England appeared on grand internal monuments, such as that designed by Robert Adam for Sir Nathaniel Curzon at Kedleston in 1763.[18] Patrons such as Sir Brooke Boothby (translator of Rousseau and the man of Sensibility *par excellence*) were precocious in their demand for the chaste correctness of eared sarcophagi:[19] the two monuments he commissioned for his parents and daughter in Ashbourne church, Derbyshire, (a cast of the latter, by Banks, graced the basement at Lincoln's Inn Fields) in the 1790s far surpass the average outdoor tomb of the day in terms of antique correctness, as well as emotional intensity. Soane's strigillated sarcophagus to Elizabeth Johnston of 1784 (IV) in Kensington was also advanced in its mass and heavy simplicity.

Rome was littered with ancient tombs. These, together with its overwhelming sense of decayed grandeur, made both Shelley and Chateaubriand see it as a city built on bones. One of the best known of classical tombs was the so-called sarcophagus of Marcus Agrippa, a giant porphyry receptacle (actually not a sarcophagus, but a basin from a public baths) that was incorporated into Clement XIII's tomb in S. Giovanni in Laterano in the 1730s. This was copied fairly closely for a

Fig. 6 Monument to George Wood (d. 1811), St Mary's churchyard, South Woodford, London Borough of Redbridge

Coade stone monument in South Woodford churchyard, erected in 1812 in memory of George Wood (d.1811) (fig. 6).

Geometric austerity was another of the principal characteristics of the neoclassical monument. The impact this had upon chest tombs can be judged from the pair of tombs illustrated in fig. 7 which stand in Wimbledon churchyard. On the right is the tomb of Thomas Walker (d.1748);[20] the neoclassical sarcophagus on the left covers the grave of Field Marshal Thomas Grosvenor (d.1834). The differences are slight but telling: the convex ends, fielded panels and Rococo cartouches of the former are renounced by the latter, which clings to the precedent of a Roman eared sarcophagus. Adherence to antique prototypes demanded some restraint: severity of form was one of their enduring characteristics.

Fig. 7 Monuments to (left) Field Marshall Thomas Grosvenor (d. 1834) and (right) Thomas Walker (d. 1748), St Mary's churchyard, Wimbledon, London Borough of Merton

Something greater than direct imitation can be discerned too. Side by side in the exceptionally appointed churchyard of St Mary's, Wimbledon, stand two aristocratic tombs. The older was erected to Margaret, Countess of Lucan, who died in 1814, aged 74; the other commemorated her niece, Lady Georgiana Quin, who died in childbirth in 1823 (fig. 8). Lady Georgiana was the daughter of the second Earl Spencer; George III and Queen Charlotte were her godparents. It is significant that both were buried in a churchyard, rather than in a more costly internal vault. Their elegiac burials in this eminently picturesque graveyard received fittingly Grecian tombs. Lady Lucan's much overgrown pile consists of a massive drum on a stepped base, above which is an equally massive triangle of Portland stone with acroteria at the angles and antefix-like finials over the shallow

pediments on each face. A smaller drum surmounts the triangle in turn; above this once stood an Ionic column supporting an urn.[21] Lady Georgiana's tomb is more conventional and better preserved. It consists of an eared chest or *arca* on a tall plinth and podium, with a delicate relief of lilies[22] on its end. This latter symbol is conventional enough in its meaning and gently classical in its emulation of a wreath. Less soothing is the huge block of Portland stone that supports the chest. Its utter lack of ornament speaks of the severity of death, and of the total separation between the living above earth and of the dead below it. Additionally, in an age of body-snatching, such precautions against tomb violation were prudent.[23] An obvious overall comparison can be drawn between the Quin tomb and the fictive tomb within the portrait of Colonel St George that was touched

Fig. 8 Monument to Lady Georgiana Quin (d. 1823), St Mary's churchyard, Wimbledon

Fig. 9 Monument to John Robins (d. 1831), St Mary's churchyard, Norwood, London Borough of Ealing

upon at the opening of this essay.

Another sarcophagus that invites examination is that of John Robins (d.1831) at Norwood Green, near Ealing (fig. 9).[24] Robins, a furniture maker and auctioneer who supplied Soane with numerous items, and whose house at Norwood was rebuilt by Soane, lies beneath a pile of Portland stone. The rectangular chest with its raised inscription panel in the form of a *tabula ansata*, a motif derived from Roman columbaria and familiar from Montfaucon[25] and Piranesi, stands on paired lions' feet. The Soanean touch lies in the scallop shell motifs that flank the upper structure: they echo the prominent examples on the roofline of Soane's design for houses on Regent Street,[26] an interesting instance of continuity between commercial premises and sepulchre.

Whether the tomb is actually by Soane is hard to say: not only is the absence of any references to it in Soane's Notebooks problematic, but the awkwardness of the shell finials, squashed into corners, is an infelicity that one would not expect. It is more likely to be the product of a mason steeped in Soanean details. The cramped arms and crossed palms of the middle section also argue against his direct authorship.

The tomb formula of an urn-capped sarcophagus was well established by 1830. It had been a favoured type of the mid-eighteenth century, as the elegant example in Harefield churchyard, Hillingdon, to John Truesdale (d.1780) demonstrates (fig. 10). This possesses a Chambers-derived French daintiness that is lacking in another example: the tomb at St Mary's, South

Fig. 10 Monument to John Truesdale (d. 1780), St Mary's churchyard, Harefield, London Borough of Hillingdon

Fig. 11 Samuel Robinson: monument to Edward Keepe (d. 1781), St Mary's churchyard, South Woodford, London Borough of Redbridge

Fig. 12 Detail of monument to Conquest Jones (d. 1773), St Mary's churchyard, Hendon, London Borough of Barnet

Woodford, to Edward Keepe (d.1781) (fig. 11). It is made of Coade stone,[27] and, unusually for an outdoor tomb, is signed: '*S. Robinson, Archt. Coade, Lambeth, fecit*'. Samuel Robinson (1752–1833) exhibited the design at the 1784 Royal Academy. The Woodford tomb has lost the putti that stood at the corners with inverted torches; only the ghostly outlines of their wings testify to the sentry duty they once performed. This has upset the composition, yet the tomb is still notable on several counts. One is symbolic: the late appearance on a monument of some prestige of skulls and crossbones, the impact of which was offset by the flaming urn with its snake handles.

Another count is stylistic. In the tomb's concoction of antique motifs, its combination of bones and antique fragments, there is a Piranesian flavour. A relief on the tomb of Conquest Jones (who died in 1773) in Hendon churchyard (fig. 12) shares the desolate tone of Piranesi's *Grotteschi* in its combination of bones and cinerary urn. It is hard to find instances of the direct influence of Piranesi on English neoclassical tombs: this might surprise, given the stature of the high priest of romantic classicism. Part of the explanation was given by Sir William Chambers, in a letter of 1774: 'he is full of manner, extravagant 'tis true, often absurd, but from his overflowings you may gather much information'.[28] Piranesi's richness of vision, method of presentation and emphasis on effect over evidence made him a difficult source from whom to borrow. The Keepe and Robins tombs both, in small ways, show what use could be made from his 'overflowings' by the designers of neoclassical tombs as they amassed motif upon motif to enhance a tomb's monumentality.

Fig. 13 R. Day: monument to Richard Budd (d. 1824), St Matthew's churchyard, Brixton, London Borough of Lambeth

Fig. 14 Sir Robert Taylor: column in memory of Peter Godfrey (d. 1769), St Mary's churchyard, South Woodford, London Borough of Redbridge

The greatest single collection of 'overflowings' from the Antique is familiar to all South Londoners. It is the monument to Richard Budd (d.1824) in the apex of St Matthew's churchyard, Brixton, by R. Day of Camberwell (fig. 13). It was described shortly after its completion as 'the finest sepulchral monument in the open air in the metropolis and perhaps not equalled by any one in the kingdom'.[29] It is a mason's masterpiece: the six-stage tomb piles sarcophagus on sarcophagus and draws on Egyptian, Greek, Roman and Christian symbolism for enrichment. Here is the expression of the Antique at its richest and most Piranesian, as precedent, propriety and scale were thrown to the winds in the interest of cumulative effect. It was and remains strong meat for a sepulchre: how Pugin must have loathed it.

Neoclassicism also saw the return to more con-

ventionally antique forms of commemoration, such as the obelisk and the pillar. Another tomb in South Woodford churchyard is the singular Corinthian column of Siena marble, erected by Sir Robert Taylor in 1771 in memory of Peter Godfrey (d.1769) (fig. 14).[30] Its materials are sumptuous; its detailing eminently antique. Taylor (who owed much to the Godfrey family, a member of which was to be chief mourner at his own funeral in 1788) may have been influenced by the continental Catholic tradition of erecting votive columns: among the most celebrated was that taken by Maderno from the Basilica of Maxentius and re-erected outside S. Maria Maggiore in 1613. A monumental form used by the Greeks[31] and with a sound biblical basis as a tributary symbol which had been used upon church monuments since the early seventeenth century, the column was better known as a political or state form of memorial.[32] The Godfrey monument was highly unusual in its day: Soane's Evelyn monument of 1785 (V) was perhaps its clearest echo. Broken columns, those preferred Romantic emblems of loss and the brevity of life, became immensely popular. One of the earliest employments of the symbol was incorporated on a monument in Bath Abbey commemorating a death in 1788;[33] perhaps the most celebrated was the memorial to Wellington's A.D.C. Colonel Gordon, designed by John Buonarotti Papworth for the field of Waterloo, and exhibited at the 1816 Royal Academy. The severed column was a modern variant on an ancient theme, endowing the hallowed symbol of stability with a sharp expression of decay.[34]

Obelisks were the emblem of honour.[35] Their patently Egyptian origins gave them a hallowed sense of antiquity that overcame their appropriation for such mundane domestic uses as lamp standards, mile stones and boundary markers; they remained a potent symbol of reverence. Internal church monuments had used the motif since the mid-sixteenth century: the French-inspired tomb of Dean Nicholas Wotton in Canterbury Cathedral of c.1570 displays a large example. It returned to outdoor commemorative use early in the eighteenth century: the Coppendale monument of after 1722 in the graveyard of the Poplar Chapel (now St Matthias, Poplar) is an early instance of its sepulchral employment, while the grandest London instance of its use as a tomb form is found on the unidentified monument in St George's Gardens, which appears to be of mid-eighteenth century date and stands some 40 feet high. Taylor was almost certainly responsible for another tomb in South Woodford churchyard which includes an urn-capped obelisk,[36] and which was erected after 1761 to Thomas North (d.1747). Later obelisk tombs include the Way memorial at Acton by John Bacon junior of c. 1803. They were to become a sepulchral commonplace in Victorian cemeteries, and (like all of the principal neoclassical sepulchral standards, be they urns, columns or stelae) enjoyed considerable and enduring popularity with Nonconformists, for whom crosses were altogether too papistical. Obelisks also possessed republican connotations, and it was no coincidence that monuments erected to heroes of the cause of Reform were honoured with such monuments: the doughty Major Cartwright, 'Father of Reform' and passionate advocate of universal suffrage, who died in 1824, had an obelisk sporting a portrait medallion (now severely eroded) erected in his memory over his grave in Finchley churchyard. Virtue was felt to be best expressed through a classical monument: 'I cannot, by any stretch of the imagination, conceive any Greek or Roman virtue surpassing the public and private worth of my deceased friend', declaimed Sir Francis Burdett at a memorial rally to Cartwright.[37] Similarly, the Martyrs' Memorials erected on Calton Hill, Edinburgh and in Nunhead Cemetery during the Chartist agitation of the 1840s took the form of mighty obelisks, hewn from the toughest of stones, as befitted monuments to enduring principles and unflinching resolve.

Pyramids were always a rarer form of tomb. The tomb of Caius Cestius,[38] rather than the Egyptian originals, had a powerful influence on neoclassical designers of fantastic schemes but was scarcely approached in actuality. The obvious exception was the mausoleum at Blickling (III.5), designed by Bonomi in 1794, which looked both forward to Canova's epic monument to the Archduchess Maria Christina (d.1798) in Vienna's Augustinerkirche, perhaps the neoclassical monument *par excellence*, and back to the pyramidal archways of Vanbrugh (at Castle Howard) and Adam (at Nostell Priory). A smaller yet substantial version covers the grave of Gerard de Vesme (d.1797) in Wimbledon churchyard; its prominent acroteria and heavy vermiculation endow it with a Piranesian presence.

One other classical tomb form warrants examination: the aedicule. The Soane family tomb (XIV) is the best known of the genre. Its central stele was protected within a four-columned canopy like an altar within a temple. Just as monuments covered remains and protected them from violation, so aedicules protected those parts of tombs that performed the fundamental task of a memorial: the preservation of a name, and the defiance of Oblivion. The Soane family tomb is a very odd affair in many ways, and, as Summerson observed, 'the memory threads woven into this monument are various'.[39] And yet Soane was not working in a vacuum: some of these threads wound back to earlier examples of the aedicular tomb. One was in Hillingdon, and marked the grave of the actor and theatre manager John Rich, England's best known harlequin, who died in 1761. His tomb consisted of a very correct eared sarcophagus cover, supporting a strigillated urn, standing on ten Doric columns around an inner stone chest.[40] An entwined snake appeared in the faces of the end pediments, as though to underscore the appeal of the composition to Soane.

Another of the memory threads led to South Woodford churchyard. There, in 1800, was built the imposingly massy mausoleum of the Raikes family (fig. 15). It took the form of a cell of Portland stone, with a segmental pediment to each face; on top stood a strigillated sarcophagus. The mouldings are plain and surfaces are bare: raw masonry is the principal ingredient. The effect again is of a pocket-sized Piranesi, or a glimpsed vision of antique solemnity. Martha Raikes (d.1797) was the sister of Job Matthew, Governor of the Bank of England, who was buried here also in 1802. Matthew was a client of Soane's, whose professional services included supervision of work on the tomb and the payment of workmen's bills, but not, it seems, the design of the mausoleum since Soane's journal for 29 September 1800 made reference to 'works done by Mr Gibson'. Jesse Gibson (d.1828) seems the most likely candidate.[41] The interest of the Raikes mausoleum lies in its anticipation of the aedicular canopy of the Soane family tomb, with its heavy and flat pediments standing on rectangular corner piers.

There is no escaping Soane's prominence as a designer of monuments; nor can we forget what an important inspiration classical tombs were for him. Yet, in terms of his overall output, tombs took up a tiny amount of his time. Moreover, as we saw with the case of Job Matthew above, involvement with the erection of monuments was but part of his professional relationship with his clients. Other architects of the day were involved in this area of work too: Robert Adam, James Wyatt, C.R. Cockerell, J.B. Papworth, C.H. Tatham among others also designed several monuments. An examination of the Royal Academy exhibition catalogues also reveals how attractive the theme of the monument was to the classically-trained aspirant architect. Just as the Bacons, Flaxman and the elder Westmacott all showed many figures destined for church monuments at the Academy prior to their installation *in situ*, so architects exhibited scores of designs for mausolea, memorials and cenotaphs. The fall of Napoleon and the triumph of British arms in particular unleashed a phalanx of designs for martial monuments; its feminine equivalent was the rush of designs for monuments to Princess Charlotte following her death in 1817. Each was a manifestation of the yearning to memorialise that was such a marked characteristic of the age.

The opening in 1833 of Kensal Green Cemetery, London's most Schinkelian enclave, heralded a new era in tomb design. The Parisian cemetery of Père Lachaise offered a potent source of inspiration with its picturesque presentation, boldness of scale and the assertively confident diversity of styles that marked its early monuments. These factors all came to be emulated by the manufacturers of monuments in the 1830s: the Egyptian style became increasingly prominent and a new exploration of scale and richness was apparent, as can be seen in the grander tombs that sprang up in Kensal Green (fig.16). The neoclassical tomb continued to flourish during the 1830s and early 1840s. What did for it, in Anglican circles at least, was the Gothic Revival. Stylistic plurality came to be seen as religious slackness under the influence of Pugin and the Oxford Movement. The result was the return in force of

Fig. 15 Jesse Gibson (?), mausoleum to the Raikes Family, c. 1800, St Mary's churchyard, South Woodford

Fig. 16 Monuments to (left) John Gordon (d. 1840) and (right) John Collett, Kensal Green Cemetery, Royal Borough of Kensington and Chelsea

the coped gravestone and the churchyard cross, and the rise of the usefully pietistic memorial such as a window or lectern.[42] Nonetheless, the classical monument remained in favour in certain quarters (especially Nonconformist ones) right up to the end of the nineteenth century, and Georgian monuments even returned to favour as part of the Queen Anne revival: hence the architect Richard Norman Shaw (d.1912) lies at rest below a perfect replica of an early Georgian tomb chest in Hampstead churchyard. The swan-song of the classical tomb was sounded by the architects of the Imperial War Graves Commission and their European counterparts.[43]

The period of Soane's lifetime was an important one for outdoor tombs: they rose in status, they became far more numerous, and the inspiration of romantic classicism greatly expanded the variety and quality of the English churchyard memorial. It is a long way from the strict conventions of the mid-eighteenth century graveyard to the plurality and opulence of Kensal Green. Soane's tomb designs knew few rivals in their day, and remain the best known today. They form the crest of a wave: but it was a wave that rose on the deeper swell of romantic classicism, and which drew its ultimate strength from the enduring monuments of the classical elegiac tradition.

I wish to thank Nicholas Penny for his helpful criticisms of an earlier draft, and Geoffrey Fisher and Philip Ward-Jackson for their photographic assistance.

1 See Penny, 1977; Whinney, (2nd ed.), 1988

2 See Colvin, 1991

3 A French popular print by G. Scheffer of c.1820 from the series '*Ce qu'on Dit et ce qu'on Pense*' neatly captures sepulchral insincerity. A young widow taking breakfast with her beau below the portrait of her gruff dead husband is shown a design for a sarcophagus to his memory: '*Il laisse une veuve inconsolable*' is her preferred inscription

4 F. H. Hart, *History of Lee* 1882, p. 17

5 John Harris *The Parish of Erith in Ancient and Modern Times*, 1885, p. 29. The urn originally stood in the garden of Belvedere House, and was moved into the new church of All Saints, Belvedere (now in the London Borough of Bexley) in 1858

6 See Llewellyn, 1995, pp. 147–62

7 C. F. Bell, ed., *Annals of Thomas Banks*, 1938, p. 187

8 See Curtz and Boardman, 1971, and Toynbee, 1971. One should remember that large mausolea and catacombs both contained internal Roman monuments, however.

9 This changing point of view is discussed in Bowdler, 1995

10 See Crossley, 1921, pp. 73 and 105

11 London County Council, *Survey of London*, xxiv, 1952, pp. 77–9; Bowdler, 1995. The burial ground is located off Wakefield Street in Bloomsbury, and is a public park known as St George's Gardens

12 Sussex's glimpse of the royal vault during the burial of William IV had put him right off such a resting place for himself; he was a Progressive in politics, and may well have wished to distance himself - even in death - from his brothers. His masonic beliefs too contributed to his desire for an outdoor resting place. See Curl, 1991, p. 207

13 Burgess, 1963, remains the best overall survey

14 See Alison Kelly, *Mrs Coade's Stone*, 1990, ch. 15

15 Tombstone studies are far more advanced in the United States: Allan I. Ludwig's *Graven Images*, Middletown, Ct. 1966, is among the best books on the subject. Scottish tombstones have been well treated in Betty Willsher and Doreen Hunter, *Stones*, Edinburgh and Vancouver, 1978

16 Illustrated as pl. 14 of Bolton, ed., 1929

17 Julian Litten's *The English Way of Death*, 1991, is the essential introduction to the history of burial

18 King, 1991, pp. 365, 368; Rysbrack was responsible for its execution

19 Penny, 1977, 20–21 and 115–16

20 The epitaph contains a rich instance of sepulchral social climbing: Walker, Surveyor-General to H.M. Land Revenue, 'was an intimate friend of Sir Robert Walpole and his portrait was introduced in a picture at Strawberry Hill'

21 James Thorne, *Handbook of the Environs of London*, 1874, p. 704

22 See Penny, 1977, pp. 31–2 on this poignant symbol

23 The body-stone was the clearest manifestation of this fear of grave violation: heavy coffin-shaped or cylindrical blocks of stone placed above the burial shaft began to be added to headstones in the early decades of the nineteenth century

24 Guillery, 1987, pp. 181–9

25 Bernard de Montfaucon's *Antiquité Expliquée* was translated by David Humphreys and published in 1721-5. Its engravings (largely taken from Boissard and Bartoli), if clumsy, provided a vast repertoire of classical motifs that architects and designers were slow to exploit

26 Stroud, 1961, cat. 183

27 Kelly, 1990, p. 243. The monument was repeated for the tomb of Martha Chivers (d.1807), West Tarring, Sussex

28 Quoted in Wilton-Ely, 1978, p. 60

29 Thomas Allen, *History of Lambeth*, 1826, p. 414. Day also signs an impressive Grecian tomb to Richard Shawe (d.1816) in Dulwich's Old Burial Ground. He did much work at Buckingham Palace and was described by Nash as 'an extraordinarily excellent workman': Gunnis, 1954, p. 123

30 Arthur Harrison, 'The Family of Godfrey of Woodford, Essex and of East Bergholt, Suffolk', *Woodford and District Historical Transactions*, xii (n.d.), pp. 3–12

31 Curtz and Boardman, 1971, p. 129

32 Yarrington, (1980) 1988, pp. 15–33

33 Penny, 1977, pp. 29–31. The tomb, by Thomas King of Bath, commemorated Robert Walsh

34 Cesare Ripa's emblem of Time included a broken column as part of the ravages wrought by Time the Destroyer: *Iconologia*, Rome 1603, p. 482. There were four English editions of Ripa during the eighteenth century

35 On obelisks as funerary emblems, see Colvin, 1991, pp. 340–44. The earliest non-sepulchral monumental obelisk erected in England was that in Ripon Market Place of 1702: see Richard Hewlings, 'Ripon's Forum Populi', *Architectural History*, 24, 1981, pp. 39–52

36 See the drawing in Taylorian Institute, Oxford (ref. ARCH. TAY. 1, f. 48)

37 F. D. Cartwright, *The Life and Correspondence of Major Cartwright*, 1826, II, p. 202

38 Colvin, 1991, pp. 72–3

39 Summerson, 1990, p. 135

40 Photographs of middling quality in the National Monuments Record, dated 1952. The tomb has since lost its urn and columns, so the aedicular effect is destroyed and the cover balances heavily on the chest

41 Gibson is himself buried in Wimbledon churchyard, below a Grecian chest with incised Soanean ornament of the sparest sort

42 See the significantly titled *Remarks on English Churches, and on the Expediency of Rendering Sepulchral Memorials subservient to Pious and Christian Uses*, Oxford 1842

43 See Curl, 1980, ch. 11

Clare Gittings

Consolation and Condolence on the Death of Mrs Soane

I know by experience how little the consolatory addresses by friends, particularly when at a distance, can add to the comfort, or subtract from the grief of one as deeply afflicted as You must necessarily be. It is however the duty of a friend to offer condolence ...   R. Burdon, Esq. to John Soane, Esq. Feb: 3, 1816.[1]

Mrs Soane died on 22 November 1815 when her husband was 62 years old. On 1 December, Soane recorded in his pocket book: 'melancholy day indeed! The burial of all that is dear to me in this world, and all I wished to live for'.[2] As news of his loss spread among his friends, those 'at a distance' were moved to write letters of condolence, which Soane preserved. They provide a fascinating cross-section of expressions of sympathy in early nineteenth-century England, a period little studied by historians of death, and are revealing for the oblique insights they give into the character of John Soane during the most profound crisis of his life. The sentiments expressed in these letters can be divided into the two types suggested by Burdon – 'consolatory addresses' and 'condolences'.

Soane kept few copies of his own letters, nor did he record verbal condolences. He had, however, a considerable circle of correspondents at this time. The most aristocratic were patrons who were also friends, such as Lady Bridport or Lady Liverpool, youngest daughter of his former patron, the Bishop of Derry. Several of his friendships dated back to his days as a young man. Travelling in Italy in 1779 he met Reginald Burdon and Sir John Coxe Hippesley on the Grand Tour. Burdon later became MP for Sunderland, and Coxe Hippesley also had a parliamentary career.

Soane made other lifelong friends in the various architects' offices in which he learned his trade. George Dance had been his master, while Soane met Richard Holland when they both worked for Richard's cousin Henry Holland.

Other later architect friends included the eccentric James Spiller, Thomas Leverton of Bedford Square, and Joseph Gandy. Among the non-architect friends was James Perry, proprietor and editor of the *Morning Chronicle* (fig. 1). He had particular compassion for Soane's bereavement, having earlier in 1815 lost his own wife at the age of 42; on a voyage from Lisbon she was captured by Algerian pirates and, although later rescued, the experience killed her.

Soane's many female friends included two young women associated with Richard Holland: Holland's niece, Mary Bradley, to whom Soane was godfather, and her friend Nora Brickenden (fig. 2). Nora, 'a romantic lady ... turned thirty', was disliked by Mrs Soane.[3] More to her taste was Barbara Hofland (fig. 3), novelist and wife of an impecunious painter. Mrs Hofland on occasion infuriated Soane; by her own admission she was 'an enthusiast or nothing'. She remained a friend, though not quite so close as was implied by her claim to Soane 'to have seen further into your heart than any'.[4]

Much of the consolatory advice offered to Soane by his friends will be familiar to anyone who has received letters or words of condolence today. How Soane reacted to their various suggestions provides some evidence of his state of mind, which inevitably had an impact on his professional life. Present-day studies of grieving reveal a number of factors which indicate the likelihood of problems in bereavement; several of these are applicable to Soane.[5] His quarrels with his sons, coupled with

Fig. 1 Richard Dighton, *James Perry* (National Portrait Gallery, London)

wrote 'to expostulate on Christian principles against unbounded sorrow', extolling the 'lessons' given by 'divine mercy'. When Soane consulted him on an inscription for Mrs Soane's monument, Burdon tried to lead him away from Virgilian fatalism to a more positive 'Greek verse, "the best of earthly goods a man possesses is a good wife."' However, Burdon's preferred choices came from the Bible, with particular suggestions from *Proverbs* and *Ecclesiasticus*. His letter ends with the warning that we have 'incalculable ages to pass with those we have loved, in a higher state of Existence, if we render ourselves <u>fit associates</u>'.[7]

Lady Liverpool sent Soane '<u>that</u> which has soothed the anguish of many an afflicted heart under a trial similar to yours' – a booklet by the evangelical preacher Richard Cecil called *A Friendly Visit to the House of Mourning*.[8] Cecil's booklet suggested a God who was a 'compassionate father, faithful creator, all-sufficient friend, comforter and gracious monitor'. One passage seems particularly apposite to Soane. Cecil warns against 'nursing and cherishing our grief ... tearing open the wound afresh by images and remembrances, and thereby multiplying those pangs which constitute the very bitterness of death itself'. This was a point which several of Soane's friends were to make to him during the course of his bereavement.[9]

Although Soane remained silent on his own religious beliefs, his admiration for Rousseau, coupled with his Freemasonry, point towards Deist beliefs; a favourite phrase used by Soane was the Deist term 'The Supreme Disposer of Events'. The memorial verses for Mrs Soane, written by Mrs Hofland, have a Deist flavour. Although they mention 'heaven' and 'a better world', their 'Eternal Father' stands aloof from the minutiae of worldly existence.[10]

It may be that Soane's theological position had little connection with the ferocity of his grief: modern studies suggest limited correlation between religious belief and coping in bereavement. A Deist philosophy, such as described by Rousseau, should lead to a calm, solitary and con-

George's involvement in Mrs Soane's death, point to difficulties ahead. Soane's own relationship with his wife – Mrs Hofland said that 'Mrs Soane was everything to her husband' – may have included a very high level of dependency, adding to the stress of bereavement. Nor was Soane's personality such as to cope well with loss; Burdon described his friend as 'too eager for stormy weather'. Soane's melancholy was profound and prolonged. As late as 1831 he was wanting a portrait painted of his wife, with her dog Fanny, also long-dead, sitting on her lap.[6]

Later nineteenth-century writers seem to have tailored letters of condolence to the religious views of their recipients. This was not the case among Soane's correspondents. Reginald Burdon

templative melancholy in the face of death. For Soane, the overriding feelings on bereavement were bitterness and anguish.[11]

Benjamin Oakley, stockbroker and theatrical impresario, passed on to Soane the 'good advice [of] our friend Mr Perry', to 'seek in business, among its anxious cares, for that relief which is denied in sedentary grief'. The recently-widowed Lady Bridport urged Soane to 'rouse yourself into the exertions of ... your profession'. She, while heart-felt in her sympathy, was probably also concerned for her late husband's memorial, which Soane had yet to complete. Soane did continue with much of his architectural work, devoting considerable time to his wife's monument. However, he declined to give the Royal Academy lectures in 1816, claiming 'shock' and 'spirits too depressed'.[12]

The consolations of work were commended by Mrs Hofland, who devised a hare-brained scheme for Soane to enter Parliament by purchasing a rotten borough. She pressed her point warmly, claiming it 'seems fitting for you in every respect – 'tis a capital to the pillar of life ... Will you then, my dear Sir, deprive yourself of the stimulant called for imperiously by your sufferings?' Soane found in her 'compliments ... the blindness of friendship, but they carry no balm to a wounded mind'. Mrs Hofland was forced to conclude that the castle, which came with the rotten borough, 'must fall then, I suppose, like all my Castles in the air'.[13]

Soane's friend Sir John Coxe Hippesley advised Soane 'to go abroad for a month, if you can spare the time ... You must seek new and various company'. Soane was slow to avail himself of the consolations of travel. It was not until 1819 that he ventured abroad, to Paris; he seems to have been greatly cheered by the experience. In the summer of 1816 he had made a visit to Harrogate and even that lightened his mood. Gandy wrote advising him which buildings to see, while Dance encouraged Soane to have 'more excursions' and 'to court dissipation in every innocent shape'.[14] The intellectual stimulus of these architectural tours was one of the few things that really seemed to

Fig. 2 Clara Maria Pope, *Nora Brickenden* (SM)

offer Soane some consolation.

A very traditional form of consolation – that provided by descendants – was denied to Soane. John Soane junior attended his mother's funeral accompanied by his wife, whom Soane later blamed for John's abandonment of architecture. The rift with George was total. James Spiller, writing to Soane, described George's 'scandalous *Champion* papers' as having 'corroded Your mind; they appear indeed to have obtained an almost exclusive possession'. He begged his friend: 'Let me conjure you to turn away from [this] constant meditation'. Soane, however, did the opposite. Four years later, in 1820, James Perry was still trying to persuade Soane to forgive George, arguing that 'there is no enjoyment on this earth so sweet as mercy'. Soane remained implacable. When another friend suggested removing the framed *Champion* articles (I.5) from his dressing

Fig. 3 Edward Finden, *Barbara Hofland* (National Portrait Gallery, London)

room, Soane replied, 'I hang those there precisely in order that I may not forget'.[15]

Soane's obsession with what he perceived as George's responsibility for his wife's death distorted the natural course of his grieving. By endlessly returning to the manner of her death, Soane failed to allow his grief to progress from the early stages of bereavement. It left him with an overwhelming sense of loss coupled with an inability to accept the reality of her death, as if he had become frozen in the initial phase of mourning. In September 1816 he wrote to Mrs Hofland:

I am more convinced every hour of the irretrievable loss I have sustained, a loss which has left a vacuum that can never be filled, and to which time cannot administer any lenient remedies.

Perry took the bold step of sitting in the place Soane reserved for Mrs Soane at the table, 'to break through a custom so prejudicial to your own happiness'. The effect on Soane is unknown, but Perry felt it necessary to write justifying his actions.[16]

Mrs Leverton, whose architect husband was ill, attempted to console Soane with the idea that 'the remembrance of superior worth is to be used as a cordial'.[17] In fact, Soane seems to have been remarkably uninterested in the inscriptions which would commemorate Mrs Soane's 'superior worth', or at least was prepared to rely on Mrs Hofland for these. This is more surprising since one was to be engraved on the monument which itself was consuming so much of his energy. The resulting inscribed tribute to Mrs Soane was similar to many others of the period, extolling her 'virtue', 'piety', 'integrity' and 'manners' (see XIV.9).

When the monument to Mrs Soane was completed in June 1816, Soane was reluctant to visit it. Mrs Hofland wrote to encourage him, citing the monument as another traditional consolation, 'the consciousness that you have left nothing undone which could evince your esteem and affection for her you loved'. Mrs Hofland herself found the monument 'exceedingly beautiful and appropriate' in its 'dignified simplicity and solid character'. She was sure Soane would 'feel some satisfaction from witnessing the fulfilment of your wishes in its appearance'.[18]

Among the many drawings for the design of the tomb are a few which show a skeleton 'hurling a spear at the marble monument' (fig. 4), like Roubiliac's Nightingale tomb in Westminster Abbey and, more distantly, Bernini's Pope Alexander VII in Rome.[19] There are two very strange aspects to this. One is to find a skeleton at all in a drawing for a neoclassical monument; the other is the positioning of the skeleton within the design. As Winckelmann had pointed out in 1776, skeletons were not used in classical times as emblems of death and very rarely appear in classical art.[20] Mrs Hofland, in her additions to the description of Soane's house, deplored 'the most revolting forms and appalling circumstances connected with our dissolution' being used as images of death, preferring 'an extinguished torch'; Soane presumably endorsed her sentiments.[21] The combination of a skeleton with neoclassical imagery possibly seems less jarring if the monument is read in terms of its Masonic symbolism.[22] However, the skeleton remains a very old-fashioned, baroque element in an otherwise avant-garde design.

The positioning of the skeleton is particularly bizarre. Soane proposed that this visually striking figure of death should be placed at the rear of the monument, invisible from the front. One of the few drawings by Soane himself for the monument shows it clearly in this position, as does Gandy's watercolour. The aedicule, as it stands today, is inscribed on three sides, each devoted to one member of the family – Soane himself on the front, Mrs Soane and John Soane junior on the sides. There is a fourth side, the back, left blank and a fourth family member not present – George Soane. It is on this blank face of the aedicule that Soane proposed to place the skeleton attacking the monument. It is tempting to read this as a representation of George's destruction of his family, a concept inexpressible in classical visual imagery, forcing Soane to resort to the baroque symbolism of a skeleton with a spear.

Mrs Hofland was the only person tactless enough to write to Soane suggesting remarriage as a consolation in bereavement, even adding: 'I have never yet been acquainted with one man, who buried a <u>good</u> wife, that did not marry again!' Soane was extremely cross, replying that, 'I can almost fancy the moon comes nearer the earth than she was wont to do, and makes men (aye and women too) mad'.[23]

In fact, when she thought Soane might really be romantically involved with another woman – she suspected Nora Brickenden, though it was actually his goddaughter Mary Bradley whom Soane had innocently met in Harrogate – Mrs Hofland became agitated for Soane's reputation. She warned him that rumours might 'spread like wild-

Fig. 4 Soane, *Soane Family Tomb – Perspective* (XIV.8 – detail)

fire' and to think of 'the horrible swallowing of the long life of honour and probity in those diabolical waves'. She explained she wished only for a suitable woman 'who could head your table at some times,' but feared that 'either you must by and bye marry ... or ... be ... subject to remarks'. Being, like his friend James Perry, 'determined never to admit a second partner to my breast', Soane solved these problems, and his troubles with servants, by appointing as housekeeper Mrs Conduitt, who later became the first Inspectress of the museum.[24]

Mrs Hofland was not always so cross in her judgments. She wrote to Soane: 'If ever there was a man to whom the intercourse of friendship is absolutely necessary, to whom it is the air, the food, the very essential part of existence, you are the man'. Soane himself admitted, in September

1816, that 'the correspondence of my friends is now almost my only consolation'.[25] Mrs Hofland's wilder schemes, and the more patient but persistent advice given by his other friends, reflect Soane's failure to conform to the currently acceptable pattern of grieving.

The Deist view of the world, in which the Deity was a remote, non-interfering figure, required a new basis for morality, not dependent on a constantly judgmental God. Such philosophical schemes had been explored by Shaftesbury, Hutcheson and Hume; they were elaborated by Adam Smith in his *Theory of Moral Sentiments*, which was first published in 1757 and ran through many subsequent editions. Smith's theory presents various philosophical difficulties, but it shaped the outlook of many who sought explanations for good and evil outside those offered by the Church. The central notion in the work of Smith and his fellow philosophers was that of sympathy. His has been called the first sociological text, since he postulates sympathy as the force which holds society together.[26] Smith uses the term sympathy 'to denote our fellow-feeling with any passion whatever', not just 'the sorrow of others'. However, he tends to speak of 'the spectator' and 'the sufferer', and his ideas underlie the role of condolence during this period.[27]

According to Smith, the spectator must 'endeavour to put himself in the situation of the other'; Hume describes human 'passions' as 'contagious'.[28] As Smith admits, 'the emotions of the spectator will still be very apt to fall short of the violence of what is felt by the sufferer'. Because of this, the sufferer, seeking that fellow-feeling with the spectator which 'constitutes his sole consolation' must

> lower ... his passion to that pitch in which the spectators are capable of going along with him. He must flatten ... the sharpness of its natural tone, in order to reduce it to harmony and concord with the emotions of those who are about him.[29]

Smith acknowledges that in 'excessive grief ... a prodigious effort is requisite before the sufferer can bring down his emotions to complete harmony and concord with those of the spectator'. Soane's friends initially 'have indulgence' for Soane's plight, till it becomes clear that he is making no efforts to control his grief, but rather fuelling it. With Smith, they agree that 'society and conversation ... are the most powerful remedies for restoring the mind to tranquility'.[30] Oakley told Soane: 'I have found great consolation in the solicitude of my friends', while Mrs Hofland and James Perry both begged Soane to 'mix' more in society.[31]

Of Soane's correspondents, Mrs Hofland came nearest to paraphrasing Adam Smith's arguments, while urging Soane to remarry:

> Every human being, who can excite a strong interest in another, proves that he is capable of feeling one; and so long as the capability exists, he is bound to the world by the common sympathies of his nature ... He may be wretched but he is not helpless. It is not the sorrow which is acute but that which stupefies, which renders us incapable of consolation ... I know what you can feel, if you would endeavour to do it.[32]

Soane evidently made greater efforts to be less aloof with his young female friends; throughout his life, women formed an important part of his circle of friends. Interestingly, Soane chose to ignore his wife's strictures on Nora Brickenden, and their friendship flourished during Soane's bereavement. Nora wrote ecstatically to Soane after the resumption of his architectural lectures in 1817: '"What shall Cordelia do? Love, and be silent". Thus I said to myself at the Royal Institution'. But, of course, she did not remain silent, mingling admiration for his lectures with personal devotion, claiming 'our friendship' to be of a 'peculiar and sacred nature', and that 'your favourite Rousseau would have understood me'.[33] Both Mary Bradley and Mrs Conduitt, though less gushing than Nora, provided genuine comfort and support, to which Soane responded.

Soane's grief, seemingly inconsolable and unending, presented a challenge to his circle of friends. Whether they chose to adopt the tenets of evangelical Christianity or of Deism of the kind favoured by Adam Smith and Freemasonry, a major feature of both systems of thought was the reduction of grief, returning the bereaved gradually to normal social behaviour. Even those friends of Soane sharing his admiration for Rousseau, whose philosophy of death encouraged prolonged melancholy, could see that Soane was far from romantically 'tasting the joy of grief'.[34] Soane's bereavement, because of his own psychological make-up and the particular circumstances of his wife's death, did not run the accepted course within the usual period of time. Soane found himself outside the norms of socially acceptable grieving for his day. It is testimony to the strength of his friendships that his correspondents persevered with him, though often exasperated and rebuffed, until his lengthy mourning finally began to abate.

FOOTNOTES

1 Bolton, 1927, p. 218

2 Bolton, 1927, p. 206

3 Quoted in Stroud, 1983, p. 96; Stroud, 1983, Bolton, 1927, and Ruffinière Du Prey, 1982, give biographical details of Soane's correspondents

4 Bolton, 1927, pp. xv and 232

5 Stroebe and Stroebe, 1987, pp. 168–223

6 Bolton, 1927, pp. 179 and 206–7

7 Bolton, 1927, pp. 218–19; Garland, 1989, pp. 154–6

8 Bolton, 1927, p. 208

9 Cecil, n.d., pp. 57–58, 60 and passim (the copy in Soane's library)

10 Bolton, 1927, pp. xiv and 222–3

11 Stroebe and Stroebe, 1987, pp. 192–4; McManners, 1981, pp. 344–5

12 Bolton, 1927, pp. 209 and 220; SM Priv. Corr. XIII H 29

13 Bolton, 1927, pp. 231, 233 and 235

14 Bolton, 1927, pp. 216, 229 and 243

15 Bolton, 1927, pp. xv, 217 and 312

16 Bolton, 1927, pp. 233 and 311

17 Bolton, 1927, p. 217

18 Bolton, 1927, p. 221

19 Summerson, 1978, p. 153

20 Cited in Irwin, 1981, p. 142

21 Soane, 1835, p. 28

22 Curl, 1991, pp. 211 and 244

23 Bolton, 1927, pp. 238–9

24 Bolton, 1927, pp. 237–8 and 312

25 Bolton, 1927, pp. 233–4

26 For further discussion of Smith's moral philosophy see Campbell, 1971; Schor, 1994, pp. 34–40; Skinner, 1970, pp. 17–29

27 Smith, 1976, p. 10. Soane did not own a copy of the *Theory of Moral Sentiments*, nor did he cite Smith in his lectures (I am most grateful to Susan Palmer for this information)

28 Smith, 1976, p. 21; Hume quoted in Schor, 1994, p. 33

29 Smith, 1976, pp. 21–2

30 Smith, 1976, pp. 23 and 45

31 Bolton, 1927, pp. 208, 234 and 312

32 Bolton, 1927, p. 233

33 Bolton, 1927, pp. 247–8

34 Bolton, 1927, p. 221

IOH.B.EPISCOPVS.MYNDENSIS
ANT.CANOVAE
FRATRI.DVLCISSIMO.ET.SIBI
VIVENS.P.C.

III·ID·OCTOB·MCMXXII

ANTONIO CANOVAE
QVI PRAESTANTIS INGENII VIM ANIMI MAGNITVDINEM
OMNEM DENIQVE VITAM AD ARTEM EXCOLENDAM INTENDIT
ITALIAE MVNICIPIA PROVINCIAE
OPIFICI PROPE DIVINO
ANNO POST EIVS OBITVM CENTESIMO

Canova's tomb, the Tempio, Possagno

52

Giles Waterfield

Dulwich Picture Gallery: An Artist's Shrine?

The combination at Dulwich of picture gallery and mausoleum has always been peculiarly arresting. It is a rare combination, in which the presence of the founders' tombs within the Gallery became crucial to its character, as Soane addressed the novel problems posed by the purpose-built art gallery. The aim of this essay is to look at the tradition of the artist's tomb; to consider analogous institutions, where the artist-founder is buried within his museum; and to study the process through which the architect arrived at the pre-eminent place of the mausoleum within this Gallery. I wish to suggest that at Dulwich Soane created a memorial of a very particular type: a building that is both a 'donor-memorial' (in the contemporary phrase) and an individual monument to artistic excellence.

The term 'donor-memorial', applied to a cultural institution where the benefactor is buried with his or her possessions, is of relatively modern coinage, and has recently been discussed in detail by Carol Duncan.[1] But in the context of the museum of art that was then emerging in Europe, the emphasis placed on the donor or instigator of a collection would not have been unfamiliar. In the relatively few contemporary museums of art in Europe – mostly national galleries derived from royal collections – some analogies can be found. These early museums did not include memorials to their founders in the form of tombs, but in most instances they presented to the visitor, as the first image with which he or she would be confronted, a statue or portrait of the founder. Thus at Düsseldorf, one of the earliest 'public' museums, where the Electoral Gallery was established in 1710 with the princely collections housed in a

purpose-built palace, a statue of the founder of the collection, the Elector Johann Wilhelm of the Palatine, was erected in the courtyard, while inside, busts of the elector and electress were placed on either side of the doors leading to the galleries.[2] At Vienna, the Belvedere Palace opened in 1781 with its collections arranged in a newly systematic historical manner: again, the visitor was confronted on arrival by portraits of the Archduke Leopold William, who had created the collection, and the Emperor Charles VI, who had enlarged it.[3] In Britain, where museums developed very differently through private patronage, the earliest institutions generally paid tribute to their private-citizen founders through portraits: at the Ashmolean Museum, which opened in 1683, a portrait of Elias Ashmole presided over the principal hall from the earliest days. In these cases, where the donor might expect to be buried in an ecclesiastical building loaded with significance, the more extreme commemoration of interment in, or beside, a museum would hardly be considered. Only in a more overtly secular age, where the foundation of museums was less closely associated with hereditary power, did the donor-memorial prosper. As Duncan has demonstrated, such memorials were to flourish especially in the United States in the twentieth century (she quotes, among others, the Huntingdon Museum and the Getty Museum).[4] In this context Dulwich, by virtue of the ambitions of its founders, can be interpreted as a rare early forerunner of a plutocratic modern type, exhibiting not only the tombs of its founders but their painted likenesses and, within the mausoleum, their portrait busts.

I would like to suggest, however, that Dulwich

Picture Gallery can with equal appropriateness be placed in another category of memorial, a category that reflects the ambiguous status of its prime founder, at the same time collector, art dealer, and artist. This category might be described as the artist's memorial, to distinguish those museums which are devoted to the memory of a particular artist and which in extreme cases include his tomb within the museum, from both the 'donor-memorial' and the artist's house, preserved as a place of pilgrimage. The latter has been aptly defined by Anthony Burton as the 'artistic shrine'.[5] The birthplace or dwelling of creative artists has been venerated since classical times. The houses of Petrarch and Dante were visited from an early date, and their tombs were also respected, that of Dante in Ravenna being regarded with particular awe. In the field of the visual arts, the house of Michelangelo in Florence, the Casa Buonarroti, was converted by his nephew into a memorial to him after his death, including a gallery commemorating his life and achievements. This tradition, particularly strong in Italy, was given a new direction with the burial of Raphael in the Pantheon: here a great artist was not only accorded an important tomb but was buried in a church with strong funerary associations. Raphael gave instructions for the creation in one of the ancient tabernacles of the Pantheon of an altar, over which a marble statue of the Virgin Mary would be placed, with his remains in the base of the statue and behind the altar,[6] emphasising the Christian aspects of burial rather than the artist's achievements. The creation of so prominent a grave for an artist, as the first layman to be buried in the building, was in itself a remarkable phenomenon, requiring permission from the Pope.

This precedent was followed in Italy to a limited extent, primarily in the Pantheon itself. From 1542 the Society of Virtuosi had their burial chapel there, creating a number of artists' monuments, while the tomb of Raphael was followed by other comparable monuments in the main body of the church, notably that of Annibale Carracci.[7]

This tomb was of particular importance: the Accademia di San Luca, the society of artists, regarded its prominence within the Pantheon as an assertion of Annibale's position as successor to Raphael. The building was well-known to Soane, who frequently used it as an illustration to his lectures.

The status of the Pantheon as the resting-place of great artists became more firmly established in the late eighteenth century – if only temporarily. The man most immediately involved in promoting this idea was the sculptor Antonio Canova (1757–1822).[8] Canova's approach to the burial of artists, including himself, and the complex relationship between his aspirations and the reservations expressed by Church leaders, make a revealing comparison with Soane's activities. From 1776 onwards it became the custom to display the busts of Italians notable for their achievements in the arts within the Pantheon, a custom that Canova fostered, commissioning at his own expense busts of famous Italians for this sanctuary of genius. As Philipp Fehl has shown, by 1820 the building contained over 60 busts as well as other memorials and 'must have served at once as a church, a museum, and a hall of fame'.[9] Such a mingling of the sacred and the profane – and one might add, so powerful a statement of nascent Italian nationalism – proved unacceptable to the Pope, who in 1820 ordered the removal of all the commemorative busts to a new gallery on the Capitol, the Promoteca Capitolina. This installation, organised in the emerging style of the new museum on chronological lines, represented a development in the commemoration of famous artists. The busts were placed in eight rooms, with a gallery of famous foreigners who had perfected their art in Rome followed by four rooms showing Italian artists from the thirteenth to the nineteenth centuries, and followed (in smaller numbers) by representatives of the other arts.[10] The Promoteca typified the secularisation of commemoration, as Dulwich had already, arguably, done on a small scale. This conflict in the nineteenth century over whether the context of a memorial should be sacred or secular, may be compared with the history of Ste Geneviève in Paris, which between 1791 and 1885 changed its status on no less than five occasions from church to pantheon and back again.

The idea of an assembly of statues of a nation's Great Men was paralleled in Italy and elsewhere. In Santa Croce in Florence a comparable if rather smaller-scale programme of memorials to great men of the arts was carried out in the early nineteenth century, with the involvement of Canova; while in Venice a scheme was devised in the late 1790s for the creation of a major memorial intended to mark the grave of Titian and, again, designed by Canova. In pre-Revolutionary France the most remarkable example was the commissioning from 1777 onwards for the Crown by the Comte d'Angiviller, superintendant of royal buildings, of a series of sculptures of Great Men of France. In this context, artists were represented by few names (only a sculpture of Nicolas Poussin was actually executed) among the statesmen and writers.[11] During the early stages of the Revolution, in 1791, it was decided that the church of Ste Geneviève should house the remains of the great men of France: again, artists were to play a subsidiary role. In Germany, projects for memorials to great men and women, including Friedrich Gilly's celebrated proposal for a monument to Frederick the Great, culminated in the creation, from 1830 to 1842, of the Walhalla at Regensburg by Leo von Klenze for King Ludwig I of Bavaria, for whom this had been a dream since his youth 30 years before. In Britain these ideas were realised in a less stirring way. The scheme, initiated in 1794, to create a collection of statues of great Britons in St Paul's Cathedral did include among the first of those commemorated as benefactors of the English people, Sir Joshua Reynolds, father of the British school (as he was thought to be) and founder-President of the Royal Academy, but the monuments were soon to be devoted primarily to soldiers and sailors.

Various though these schemes were, they all, naturally, reflected emergent concepts of nationalism. They tended to be created at times of political tension, and to give the greatest attention to warriors and statesmen, with philosophers and other writers also quite well represented. But the idea of emphasising creative artists, and especially painters and sculptors, seems to have been unique to Italy (and, in one instance, Denmark). This development is not surprising when the growing sense of the identity of an Italian nation was fostered by the publication in the late eighteenth century of a series of early works of art history, which emphasised Italian primacy in the visual arts.

Among the prominent Italians actively involved in this process, one of the most important was, as we have seen, Canova. The tomb of this sculptor presents a particularly revealing comparison with Dulwich. One would hardly suggest a direct relationship between the two schemes, though it seems possible that Soane influenced the Italian sculptor, who visited the new gallery-mausoleum when in London in 1815. Canova's role in his own commemoration was a somewhat passive one, since he left no instructions about his burial in his will and the elaborate arrangements made were devised by others. Nevertheless, the history of Canova's tomb and museum may be seen as a complete realisation of the concept to which Soane aspired at Dulwich and which he achieved in a somewhat different form at Lincoln's Inn Fields.

In 1818 Canova instituted the building of a new parish church, to be known as the Tempio, at his birthplace at Possagno, in northern Italy (fig. 1). This circular edifice was intended to incorporate the greatest qualities of both the Parthenon and the Pantheon. On Canova's death, the remains of an artist who was regarded both as the embodiment of revived classical genius and as one of Italy's greatest sons, were divided among various interested sites. His heart (which at first had been sent to the Venetian Accademia) was placed in the church of the Frari in Venice, in an elaborate tomb on which a number of prominent sculptors collaborated, while his right hand was given to the

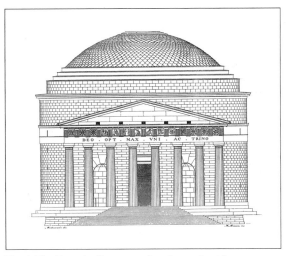

Fig. 1 The Tempio, Possagno: elevation and section

Accademia in exchange for his heart, and placed in the senate hall in a porphyry urn, with his chisel inserted into the tablet beneath. The body of the artist was taken to Possagno and buried in the Tempio. The tomb had, by a curious history, been designed by Canova in 1820 for an Italian nobleman, but was not used for that purpose and was applied to this new use. As it now exists, Canova's tomb (fig. 2), a classical sarcophagus set like that of Raphael on a relatively plain base, flanked by busts of the artist and his bishop-brother (by Canova himself), is close in conception to Soane's early designs for the Dulwich monuments. As at Dulwich, the tomb is closely related to a museum: after the artist's death, his adjacent house was converted by his brother into a gallery containing the original plasters of his major sculptures (fig. 3). Although at Possagno the museum and the tomb are housed in separate buildings, the relationship between the living art and the dead man is sharply indicated. The temple, the tomb and the museum were intended to arouse a sense of honour and patriotism in the visitor, through a powerful classical vocabulary. Canova's own concern for the commemoration of great Italians was appropriately celebrated in his own memorial.

Such artist-memorials were not common in nineteenth-century Europe, although museums

dedicated primarily to the work of a particular artist did become a relatively frequent type in the mid-nineteenth century.[12] It is worth making a comparison with the museum-memorials created for two of Soane's contemporaries, the Danish neoclassical sculptor Bertel Thorwaldsen (1760–1844) and the American history painter John Trumbull (1756–1843). Both men are buried in the museums devoted (originally, at least, in Trumbull's case) to their work: the Dane in the Thorwaldsen Museum in Copenhagen, designed by the neoclassical architect M.G. Bindesbøll, and the American in what is now the Yale University Art Gallery, New Haven. Each of these museums had a somewhat individual character, although an emphasis on the supremacy of the individual artist and a strongly patriotic character were shared.

The connection between Thorwaldsen and Canova was clear: the Danish artist constantly sought to emulate his Italian rival, and was inspired by Possagno to create a museum of his own plasters, similar to Canova's, in Copenhagen. The Thorwaldsen Museum as it now stands was begun with the sculptor's participation in the 1830s, with early schemes imitating the Tempio at Possagno. The building was completed after his death in a gesture by his compatriots (who paid

Fig. 2 (left) Canova's tomb, the Tempio, Possagno. Fig. 3 (below) Gipsotheca, Possagno

Fig. 4 (right) Thorwaldsen Museum, Copenhagen – exterior. Fig. 5 (below) Thorwaldsen Museum – courtyard and Thorwaldsen's grave.

for the work through individual subscriptions). They saw in the sculptor one of Denmark's greatest sons, and regarded the establishment of an appropriate museum as a symbol of 'the Danish spirit' as well as of nationally-shared artistic ideals.[13] The building (fig. 4), intended by Bindesbøll to be archaeologically accurate, reflected in architectural terms the correctness that the sculptor had achieved in his own work, and was seen by contemporaries as a modern equivalent to the great monuments of the classical past, a new Acropolis or Pantheon. In the central courtyard of the severe neoclassical building completed in 1848 is a slab marking the sculptor's grave (fig. 5). The burial chamber is decorated with palm leaves, roses and lilies against a blue background, illustrating a hymn inspired by the sculptor's death: 'Let go the black cross and where it stood may lilies grow'. The theme was not death but resurrection,[14] a theme reinforced in the iconographical programme in the decoration of the courtyard. The museum stands at the centre of the city, close to the Royal Palace: of this group, it is the institution most closely bound up with the apparatus of the state. It is remarkable that a museum, bearing the name and built around the tomb of an artist, should carry such a weight of meaning.

The same patriotic element, with scarcely any classical emphasis, can be seen in the foundation in 1832 of the Trumbull Gallery at Yale University (fig. 6). John Trumbull, 'Patriot-Artist' as he described himself,[15] pupil of Benjamin West, aide-de-camp to George Washington (if only for nineteen days, a point he did not emphasise), perpetrator of a series of paintings in the Capitol in Washington depicting the American War of Independence, and possessed with 'a passionate desire for posthumous fame',[16] conveyed many of his works to Yale in exchange for an annuity, on the understanding that they would be shown in a gallery designed by him and situated, perhaps significantly, close to the College Chapel.[17] The new museum was contained in two large exhibition rooms given over to Trumbull's work, with the sci-

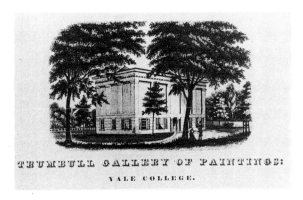

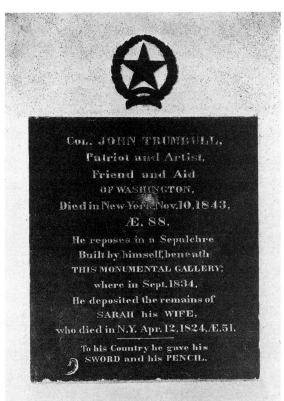

Fig. 6 (above) Trumbull Gallery, Yale University – exterior. Fig. 7 (below) Trumbull's memorial stone, Trumbull Gallery, Yale University.

entific collections beneath. The painter was buried under his museum, beside his wife, the place being marked by a black marble slab (fig. 7). An iron tablet set into the building proclaimed that the Trumbull Gallery would 'remain as long as stone iron & silver shall last, a splendid memorial to the honor of the great artist – and as a moral lesson to a distant posterity'.[18] On his death, the dual achievements of this determinedly great man were celebrated by the arrangement round the tomb of relics. Portraits of the Trumbulls hung beneath a full-length portrait of Washington,[19] while a sword captured by Trumbull in battle, and his palette and brush, were shown below. Though the Gallery came to be renamed the Yale University Art Gallery, and was moved on several occasions to other locations, Trumbull stubbornly stayed with the collections, travelling on each occasion to the new building. Although the monument to the artist-founder was much less elaborate (as befitted a republic) than those at Possagno and Copenhagen, the idea of the museum as both personal glorification of the artist and national shrine was comparable. A major difference lay in the fact that at New Haven it was the artist, and nobody much else, who was concerned with the perpetuation of his fame.

For both Soane and Noel Desenfans, the commemoration of great men, and the advancement of a nationally-organised scheme for this purpose, held particular interest. In 1799 Desenfans published his most ambitious work, *A Plan ... to Preserve Among Us, and Transmit to Posterity, The Portraits of the Most Distinguished Characters of England, Scotland and Ireland ... Without any Expence to Government*. Inspired by the statues of military heroes that were about to be erected in St Paul's, Desenfans, in what has been identified as the 'first formal proposal for a national portrait gallery',[20] advocated the commissioning of portraits of prominent British citizens. Though the scheme led to nothing, it was one that mattered to Desenfans, and that he did his best to promote through the machinations at the Royal Academy of which he and Bourgeois were so fond. For Soane too, the national commemoration of prominent individuals was of recurring interest, as his Lecture VII makes clear. There he speaks of the desirability of emulating in architecture the paintings and sculptures that record 'the splendid achievements of our illustrious Men, and the glorious transcendent exploits of our Heroes by Sea and Land',

stressing, as did many of his contemporaries, the importance of military achievement. He expressed the hope that buildings of an equivalent grandeur to the paintings and with a similar purpose would be erected in Britain, urging his listeners to avoid the reproach of foreigners and to 'imitate our Gallic neighbours, let us look at their Pantheon [fig. 8], an edifice devoted exclusively to the honor of great men'.[21] Among his imaginary schemes the national monument was one of the most frequent ideas; and one of the subtexts of his own museum at Lincoln's Inn Fields was the commemoration of the great.

It is in this intellectual climate that the Bourgeois and Desenfans mausoleum should, I believe, be viewed. Though the name of Francis Bourgeois hardly has the same resonance as that of Raffaello Sanzio, Bourgeois regarded himself as a serious painter and distinguished by his membership of the Royal Academy, and he included fifteen of his own paintings in his collection. In the style of contemporaries such as Benjamin West, the works of the present were given validity by being displayed among the undisputed masters of the past. Much of Desenfans' energy had been dedicated to the establishment of his friend's reputation as a great painter, and this energy lived on in Sir Francis. It was the collectors' original hope that their paintings would remain in their house at Charlotte Street, a building to the rear of which an ambitious elevation, designed supposedly by Robert Adam, had been added at their expense. In this building with its large collection of pictures, its skylight room with the finest works, and its chapel for the founders, an artist's and collectors' shrine was envisaged. Although Bourgeois was obliged to transfer his ambitions to Dulwich, the purpose moved with him.

The Bourgeois collection had its own commemorative aspect. Aside from the artist's paintings, it boasted a group of portraits of British artists including those regarded as among the founders of the native school: Reynolds, Gainsborough, de Loutherbourg and Opie. In the early days of the Gallery, these portraits hung in a group on the

Fig. 8 Soane, *The Pantheon, Paris* (SM)

west wall of the second room, with the portrait of Bourgeois. A tentative attempt to create a broader gallery of notable portraits may be detected in the assembly of depictions of leaders of the theatre, such as Mrs Siddons and her brothers, and of such representatives of French seventeenth-century culture as Louis XIV and Boileau. But in the absence of any statement by Bourgeois over such a purpose, or any illumination from the inscription on the tomb, it is impossible to do more than suggest such an intention.

*   *   *   *   *   *

Whatever the aims of Bourgeois other than his broadly-stated intention of creating a national collection of paintings, the involvement of Soane in this process was crucial. It may convincingly be

argued that it was Soane who gave the mausoleum the importance it has in the existing building, and who wished to create a memorial not only to his friends but to himself. The second part of this essay will examine the emphasis that Soane gave to the role of commemoration at Dulwich, and the difficulties that he encountered.

An analysis of the discussions over the new building suggests that the emerging interest in the funerary character of the building was inspired by the architect rather than the patron, Sir Francis Bourgeois, or the client, the Master, Warden and Fellows of Dulwich College. The fulfilment, or at any rate partial fulfilment, of Soane's intentions stimulated a conflict between his wishes and those of his clients, which continued long after they were all dead. It was a conflict that epitomised contrasting ideas towards death: the wish on the one hand to lay a strongly associational emphasis on the funerary building, and on the other to marginalise the tomb so that it became a peripheral space scarcely impinging on the experience of the art-lover. At the same time, it reflected the complex relationship between memorials and places of worship.

Bourgeois always intended that his remains, and those of his friends Noel and Margaret Desenfans, should lie beside the pictures they had devoted so much of their lives to accumulating. As far as Bourgeois' intentions went, one may overestimate his personal ambitions. In his final Will, dated 20 December 1810, he mentioned the 'Tomb or Sarcophagus' that he wished to be erected at Dulwich on the lines of that existing at Charlotte Street, while in his discussion with the Master of Dulwich College shortly before his death he spoke of burial in 'some little nook' or 'a little part of the chapel which he would provide for'.[22] Bourgeois' approach was more conservative than his architect's. His extension was not apparently intended to occupy a significant symbolic role within the new building. It belonged, rather, to the tradition of a private chapel added to an existing parish church, satisfying the convention that a patron should be commemorated within the appropriate ecclesiastical building. Soane referred to this role of Bourgeois as the new founder in his *Memoirs*, when he evoked Edward Alleyn, the original founder of Dulwich College, revisiting his charity and exclaiming with amazement on seeing the Gallery '"What a graft on the original stock! ... how came this splendid adjunct to be attached to my homely edifice?"'[23] Bourgeois saw his memorial as Christian, and specifically Anglican. He referred to the mausoleum at Charlotte Street as a 'chapel',[24] and Robert Corry, a Fellow of Dulwich College, was appointed to act as chaplain both there and, it was planned, at Dulwich, where the circular chamber is described on the early plans as the 'chapel'. This Christian allegiance is by no means clear today from the mausoleum, with its total avoidance of Christian symbolism, created by the Deist architect.

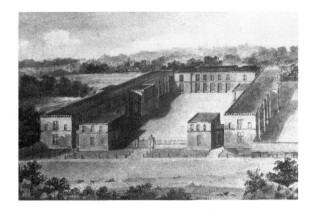

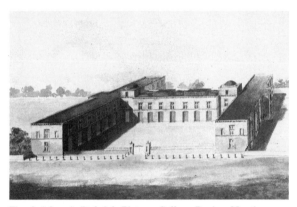

Fig. 9 (above) Dulwich Picture Gallery: Design No. 1 – perspective (SM). Fig. 10 (bottom) Dulwich Picture Gallery: Design No. 2 – perspective (SM)

The first plans produced by Soane more or less adhered to the idea of a mausoleum attached to the chapel. Following Bourgeois's intentions, one of the early drawings (Design No 1 (SM 65/4/6) dated 17 April 1811) featured a mausoleum next to the chapel (fig. 9). At this stage it was not given an independent architectural identity, even though it was a free-standing building, but was treated as a square block in the stripped-Gothic style that Soane was investigating, within the proposed quadrangle. Similar ideas applied in other early designs, with the mausoleum being for example (in Design No. 2, of the same date (SM 65/4/9)) made into part of the central stroke in an H-shaped building, occupying the ground floor of a tower between gallery and chapel (fig. 10). Although there is some anticipation in these early drawings of the eventual position of the

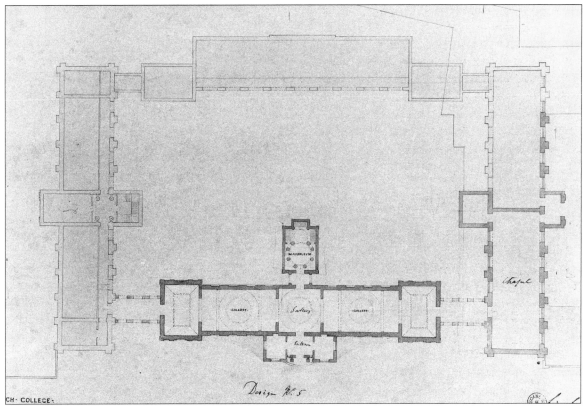

Fig. 11 Dulwich Picture Gallery: Design No. 5 – plan showing mausoleum in quadrangle (SM)

mausoleum, its position appears of relatively minor importance, and the perspectives, together with most of the elevations in a curious variety of classical-cum-Gothic styles, do not treat the tomb-chamber as a significant individual element.

Soane soon abandoned this unassuming role for the mausoleum. As early as May 1811 he proposed in Design No. 5 (SM 65/4/16) a scheme in which the mausoleum emerged for the first time as an important free-standing structure, on the quadrangle (east) side of the Gallery and at its centre, with the entrance vestibule situated opposite it (fig. 11). This was the idea to which he was to adhere for the rest of the design process, though his wishes were to be radically altered in one respect. In the scheme accepted by the College on 12 July 1811 (SM 65/4/34), the plan showed the Gallery as the west wing of the new

quadrangle (fig. 12). The almshouses that were to be part of the new building were placed on the western, outer side of the Gallery, with the mausoleum on the quadrangle side. What is striking about the designs that Soane persuaded the College to accept is that the quadrangle would have contained as its principal feature a mausoleum, situated directly opposite the principal entrance, and dominating both visually and spiritually the whole complex. It is a curious idea, and one that Soane appears to have developed on his own initiative: it suggests that the siting of the mausoleum had come to dominate his thinking about the new building. The Gallery was to be approached from the present Gallery Road by a vestibule on the east side of the building, and placed in the centre of the two wings of almshouses, with subsidiary entrances through arcades at the sides.

63

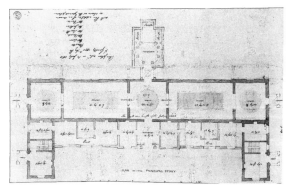

Fig. 12 Dulwich Picture Gallery: accepted plan (SM)

As we have seen, this scheme was accepted by the College authorities on 12 July. On the evidence of the ultimate decision it was not an idea they could tolerate for long:[25] and it is not surprising that unlike Soane they should have had qualms about the displacement, at least symbolically, of the College's founder by the founder of the new Picture Gallery. It is revealing that on the plan (SM 65/4/37) presented to the governing body and approved by them, the composition is shown with the mausoleum on the quadrangle side, worked out in pen and watercolour; but that freehand proposals have been added in pencil, showing the mausoleum in two less prominent positions, tucked away behind the main buildings and closer to the chapel block. A proposal for a library, to the south, was also added. One may assume that these alternatives were discussed when the plan was shown to the Fellows. At all events, in November 1811, after building had begun, the decision was made to move the mausoleum from the east to the west side of the Gallery.

This change of siting was to prevent the full realisation of the architect's intentions. Soane produced an alternative scheme for the erection of a further chamber (in some versions with a lantern comparable to that of the mausoleum, in others only a one-storey building) on the east side of the Gallery, which would have served as an entrance hall. This was never executed, but it reappeared in *Public and Private Buildings* as the ideal solution. Although internally, with the additions of 1910 the sequence of entrance vestibule (ie the present entrance hall), gallery and tomb-chamber is now experienced as Soane intended, both in the nineteenth century when the building was entered from the south end and the mausoleum was practically ignored, and even today when the incurious visitor may well enter the Gallery and leave it without experiencing the exterior of the mausoleum at all, the crucial importance of this structure risks being overlooked.

For Soane, by contrast, the mausoleum had become the central element of the new building. This was not always the case: in the earlier stages (figs. 13–15) it did not at all dominate the elevation to which it is attached. In a number of the drawings in the second stage of design (around July 1811) it is shown as scarcely higher, or no higher at all, than the Gallery behind it: for example a drawing of 24 October 1811 (SM 65/4/35) depicts it with the decoration of the scrolled pediment on the same level as the acroteria on the main block. It tended to be closely related to the rest of the building through the relationship between the archways in the mausoleum (at present occupied by the doors) and the openings in the arcade which was to run along the front of the building. The relationship between solids and voids proposed here was highly characteristic of the architect's work.[26] Nor did the present authoritative arrangement of the urns, and the manipulation of scale in the upwards sequence of cubes from the broken solidity of the lower storey, with its contrasts of light and dark, to the attic and the topmost urn, spring immediately to Soane's mind. It was a design at which he arrived with much thought: some of the earlier proposals show a squat building, decorated with a curiously un-classical triple arch intended to match the Jacobean character of the College, with a variety of finials (flaming torch, pineapple), and using motifs such as the scrolled pediment which he had applied on the Samuel Bosanquet and de

Fig. 13 (top) Dulwich Picture Gallery: elevation (SM 65/4/19). Fig. 14 (middle) Dulwich Picture Gallery: elevation (SM 65/4/36). Fig. 15 (bottom) Dulwich Picture Gallery: elevation (SM 65/4/35)

Loutherbourg tombs. One drawing, worked out in detail and presumably intended for lectures, even shows on all four corners the seated figure of Britannia, invoking the language of patriotism which played so strong a part in these memorials, but which in a mausoleum dedicated to a Frenchman and a Swiss could hardly be held to be valid.

In addition to the friendship with Bourgeois, Dulwich had a personal significance for Soane. As he put it in his *Memoirs*, the 'original design' of the new College building was to contain a library on the side of the quadrangle opposite the chapel, and 'it was once my intention, if neither of my relatives embraced the profession of an Architect, to have followed the example of my much-esteemed friend, Sir Francis Bourgeois, and have left my Library and Collection of Antiquities to the Master, Warden, and Fellows of Dulwich College.'[27] (At the time he had begun his creation of the museum at Lincoln's Inn Fields but his plans had not reached full development.) The resulting museum would have represented the principal visual arts, anticipating Soane's wish to create in Lincoln's Inn Fields a museum of architecture, painting and sculpture. Though he was frustrated in this purpose, it seems reasonable to suggest that at this early stage he may have contemplated being buried at Dulwich himself, intending the mausoleum not only for Bourgeois but for John Soane. That would explain the creation of an additional, empty, sarcophagus. The combination at Dulwich, and particularly in the mausoleum, of references to primitive, Egyptian, classical and Gothic architecture, which has recently been elucidated by Andrew Ballantyne,[28] would have been peculiarly well-fitted to an architect's memorial.

The importance of Dulwich to Soane is suggested by the drawings of Dulwich that he presented at the Royal Academy. The early ones stress the sepulchre rather than the pictures: in 1811, a 'View of a Mausoleum...' in the following year, 'Design for a mausoleum ... and a gallery', in 1813, 'Design for a mausoleum attached to the gallery now building...' and only in 1815 'View of

Fig. 16 Dulwich Picture Gallery Mausoleum from *Designs for Public and Private Buildings*

the Gallery'.[29] In Gandy's lecture drawings, it was the funerary structure that primarily absorbed the architect and his most talented draughtsman: repeatedly, the sepulchre is shown in brilliant, if often stormy, light with the gallery and almshouses in relatively low relief behind. In *Public and Private Buildings*, published in 1828, in which he published his major executed and intended schemes, Soane included the Gallery (fig. 16), with an engraving of the quadrangle scheme with the mausoleum in the centre, and another of the interior of the mausoleum with the tombs in their original splendid state (and, by a

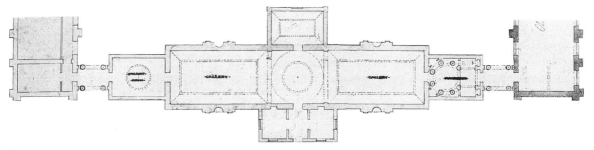

Fig. 17 Dulwich Picture Gallery: Design No. 4 – plan (detail)

curious inaccuracy, with the tomb of Desenfans in its central position as it had been at Charlotte Street). In addition, he used drawings of the Gallery in his Royal Academy lectures to illustrate constructional techniques;[30] and discussion of the building occupies a considerable part of his somewhat whimsical memoirs.

Although the mausoleum had to be built with limited funding, Soane paid close attention to the details. The '*lumière mystérieuse*' was of particular importance: in his *Memoirs* of 1835 Soane gave an impression of the effect he intended, stressing the intimate relationship between the burial space and the Gallery itself. Evoking one of the dinners for members of the Royal Academy that had been planned for the Gallery by Bourgeois, he wrote:

How gratifying to the reflective mind must such a repast be, surrounded with some of the richest treasures of the pencil! – To increase the enjoyment of this splendid scene, we have only to fancy the Gallery brilliantly lighted for the exhibition of this unrivalled assemblage of pictorial art, – whilst a dull, religious light shews the Mausoleum in the full pride of funereal grandeur, displaying its sarcophagi, enriched with the mortal remains of departed worth, and calling back so powerfully the recollections of past times, that we almost believe we are conversing with our departed friends who now sleep in their silent tombs.[31]

In this passage the writings of eighteenth-century French theorists and of proponents of the Picturesque encouraged Soane to create an imaginary picture of the building in which the contrast between death and life was to be conveyed through light.

For the interior of the mausoleum, the plan was always to reuse the scheme created at Charlotte Street. This was the declared intention of Bourgeois, and in the plan for Design No. 4 (SM 64/4/13), for example, dated May 1811, the mausoleum is shown as two chambers as it was finally to be built (fig. 17), although externally it is treated as part of the organisation of blocks around the quadrangle. The circular antechamber, with its coffered ceiling, used a form long associated with sacred buildings, but reminiscent also of the Rome Pantheon which, arguably, Soane wished to recall. The detailing, too, contained various significant references. The Roman altars outside, always planned for the exterior, emphasised the funerary character of the building, although the statues that were to stand upon them never materialised. The painting of the tombs, in their simplified state, to resemble porphyry is also of interest. Porphyry, or polished Egyptian granite, as seen in replica at Dulwich, was rare in Britain in the 1810s. The real material, quarried in specific sites in Upper Egypt, had been reserved in Ancient Egyptian times for funeral purposes and in the 1810s was scarcely available in Britain except in very small quantities – though Soane would have seen notable ancient examples such as the Sarcophagus of Constantina in the Vatican Museum.[32] His choice of the material, if only in replica, is characteristic both of his learning and of his willingness to use theatrical devices. As has often been remarked, there is no specifically Christian symbolism in the mausoleum, any more than there is in the architect's other monumental commissions.

The architect's intentions were not to the liking of the College authorities. He had intended that access from one part of the structure to the other should be unrestricted, and was appalled on revisiting Dulwich some years later to find that a grille had been erected in front of the mausoleum, preventing the visitor from entering this space. The idea of the funerary chamber as a place of public, if solemn, access, was not acceptable to the conservative clerics who formed the majority of the governing body. Entry to the burial space continued to be restricted throughout the nineteenth and early twentieth centuries, and by the beginning of the twentieth century the mausoleum was protected from the viewer by a door as well as a grille.[33] When the Gallery was rebuilt after the Second World War, a glass door was introduced, acknowledging the visual importance of the interior but not the intended relationship of the two spaces. Only in 1981 was this glass door succeeded by two doors in the manner of Soane, designed to be kept open during visiting hours and to allow the visitor to experience the original effect. In this respect Soane's intentions had, finally, triumphed.

Sir John Soane's own museum in Lincoln's Inn Fields has often been analysed in terms of its funerary character. According to precise definition, it does not belong to the genre of artist's memorial in that the architect is not buried there. On the other hand, an early drawing by Soane indicates a place for a 'Mausoleum' within the Museum, suggesting that he considered this possibility before the death of his wife and the construction of the family tomb.[33] In the end only his dog was buried in the Museum. In many respects the building resembles other artists' memorials. Throughout, drawings and models of Soane's executed and imaginary scheme reflect his fear over their mortality. The union of the arts is central to the Museum's programme, while the patriotic element which played a vital part elsewhere inspired the inclusion of representations not only of leading contemporaries but of such great Englishmen of the past as Shakespeare. The building contains numerous depictions of the architect, notably the bust by Chantrey placed in a position of honour in the Dome, and juxtaposed with Raphael and Michelangelo, surrounded by funerary urns and with the sarcophagus of Belzoni beneath. Among its many aspects, the Museum reflects Soane's sophisticated understanding of the contemporary European identification of museums with mausolea and must be seen as his memorial, without his remains but with the artist otherwise omni-present. At Dulwich the language of this discourse is less fully developed: but its mausoleum represents, nevertheless, a premonition of the architect's final creation.

FOOTNOTES

1 See J. Traeger, pp. 37–47, in Haskell 1981; and Duncan, 1995, pp. 72–101

2 *Catalogue des Tableaux Qui se trouvent Dans les Galleries du Palais de S.A.S.E. Palatine à Düsseldorf*, c. 1750

3 Christian von Mechel, *Verzeichnis der Gemaelde der K.K. Bilder Gallerie in Wien*, 1781, p. XII

4 Duncan, 1995, *op. cit.*

5 Anthony Burton 'Artistic Shrines', *Museums Journal*, 80, 3, Dec 1980, pp.141–5

6 See Tilman Buddensieg, *Raffaels Grab* in *Sonderdruck aus der Festschrift Kauffmann*, Munuscula Discipulorum 1968

7 See Z. Wazbinski, *Annibale Carracci e l'Accademie di San Luca*, in *Les Carrache et Les Décors Profanes*, Ecole Française de Rome, 1988, p. 557 ff.

8 See Philipp Fehl, *Canova's tomb and the cult of genius* in *Labyrinthos* I 1/2, 1982, pp. 46–66

9 Fehl, 1972, p. 48

10 Agostino Tofanelli, *Descrizione delle sculture, e pitture che si trovano al Campidoglio*, 1820, pp.102–29

11 See A. McClellan, *Inventing the Louvre*, 1994, pp. 82–90

12 For example, the Musée Ingres in Montauban; the Musée Fabre in Montpellier; the Watts Gallery, Compton, Surrey (where a mausoleum was also erected, in the grounds)

13 L. B. Jørgensen, 'Thorvaldsen's Museum, Symbol and Interpretation', *Meddelelser far Thorvaldsens Museum*, 1970, p. 146; and Jørgensen, 'Neoclassical Architecture in Copenhagen and Athens', *Architectural Design, 57*, 1987, p. 13

14 Jørgensen, 1970, p. 148

15 See T. Sizer, ed., *The Autobiography of Colonel John Trumbull, Patriot-Artist, 1756–1843*, 1953

16 Sizer, 1953, p. xii

17 See Sizer, 1953, p. 322ff for an account of Trumbull as an architect

18 Sizer, 1953, p. 377

19 This conjunction of the image of a museum-founder with that of a head of state or national hero represents an interesting development of the traditional founder-portrait, and has lately found striking expression in the entrance hall of the Thyssen-Bornemisza Museum in Madrid, where the King and Queen of Spain hang on the same wall as, if a little distance from, the noble founders of the museum

20 Marcia Pointon, *Hanging the Head*, 1993, p. 229

21 Bolton, *Lectures*, 1929 p. 118

22 *The Last Will and Testament of Sir Francis Bourgeois* (SM Private Correspondence, IX/D/2/2) – see Appendix

23 Soane, 1835, p.3 8

24 *The Last Will and Testament of Sir Francis Bourgeois* – see Appendix

25 Mellinghoff suggests that it was Soane who decided to change the orientation: the Private Sittings Book of Dulwich College does not make the position clear

26 See SM 15/2/2

27 Soane, 1835, p. 39

28 Ballantyne, 1994

29 He exhibited a Dulwich drawing again at the Royal Academy in 1823

30 Three drawings were used to illustrate Lecture XII

31 Soane, 1835, p. 39

32 Information from Dr Kerney of the Natural History Museum, London

33 Waterfield, 1987 p. 42

34 I am very grateful to Helen Dorey and Susan Palmer for their help over this (and many other) matters

70

The Catalogue

Giles Waterfield and Christopher Woodward

Sir John Soane

Thomas Cooley
(active first half of nineteenth century)

I.1 *Sir John Soane and John Flaxman,* 1810

The neoclassical sculptor John Flaxman (1753–1826), a close friend of Soane, served as the first Professor of Sculpture at the Royal Academy during Soane's tenure as Professor of Architecture. The character of Sir John Soane's Museum is much influenced by its inclusion of Flaxman's work and of objects formerly in his possession: notably models of famous memorial sculptures.

Pencil (215 × 126)

National Portrait Gallery, London

Antonio van Assen (d.1817)

1.2 *Mrs Soane and her Children,* c.1805

Van Assen, who aspired to create ambitious historical works in watercolour and exhibited regularly at the Royal Academy between 1788 and 1804, was employed by Soane to add figures to his architectural drawings. The Tyringham drawing (XVIIc.1) is an example of this collaboration.

Watercolour (320 × 270)

SM P305

Daniel Maclise RA (1806–1870)

I.3 *Sir John Soane,* 1836

The promising young Irish artist Maclise was recommended to Soane in 1836 by his fellow Academician, the portraitist Thomas Phillips. In 1836 Maclise painted a portrait of Soane which the artist presented to the Literary Fund, but the work did not please the sitter, who instigated its destruction. Maclise also executed this etching, which appeared in *Fraser's Magazine*. It is the last known portrayal of the architect.

Etching (232 × 180)

SM 69/3/6

I.2

I.4 *Les Confessions de J.J. Rousseau*
(with Soane's drawing of Rousseau's tomb)

The tomb of Rousseau, prophet of the Romantic sensibility, who died in 1778, was set among trees on an island at the country estate of Ermenonville, near Paris. It became a cult site. Soane included a sketch of Rousseau's tomb in one of the drawings of the family tomb at St Pancras (XIV.X). In his own copy of the *Confessions*, Soane wrote in the inscription from the tomb:

Entre ces peupliers paisibles
Reste Jean Jacques Rousseau
Approchez coeurs vraies & sensibles
Votre Ami dort sous ce tombeau.

Octavo, 1783, vol. I

Sir John Soane's Museum

I.3

I.4

I.5 'Death Blows'

Newspaper cuttings (from *The Champion*, 10 September 1815 and 24 September 1815 – reproduced by photograph) and label, prepared by Sir John Soane, and inscribed: *'Death blows given by George Soane/10th: & 24th: Sept: 1815'*.

Soane believed that these newspaper articles, which correspondence with the owner of *The Champion* revealed to have been written at least in part by his younger son George, had caused the death of his wife. The articles lament the shortage of accomplished artists and architects in Britain, 'these ill requited pursuits [being left] to men of weaker intellect and greater industry'. It mentions a number of talented figures (including the architect Robert Smirke, supposedly a co-author of the article), remarks that foreigners 'laugh at the heavy, lumbering extravagance of the Bank [of England]', and ridicules Soane's architecture as ludicrously inappropriate for its purpose. The article concludes: 'The most extraordinary instance of this perversity of taste and dullness of invention is to be found [at Lincoln's Inn Fields]. It looks like a record of the departed, and can only mean, that considering himself as defunct in this better part of humanity – the mind and its affections – he has reared this mausoleum for the enshrinement of his body'.

Soane had the articles framed and kept them on view in the house, in spite of at least one effort by his friends to persuade him to remove them. He announced his intention to leave the papers, glass and frame to George as his only bequest to his apparently extraordinarily unpleasant son. Soane especially resented the fact that his son, who had received advantages of education which had been completely denied to him, had abused these advantages with such cynicism.

Sir John Soane's Museum

Sir John Soane RA (1754–1837)
I.6 *Designs for Public and Private Buildings*

In his last major publication Soane illustrated projects, many of them unexecuted, from the whole of his career but with an emphasis on the later years. They include a number of his tombs and monuments, such as the Duke of York monument, Dulwich, Tyringham and the National Debt Redemption Office, illustrating the importance of these schemes in his œuvre. The volume concludes with engravings of the family tomb and Mrs Soane's memorial tablet, and reprints not only her epitaph but numerous verses written in her memory.

Folio, London, 1828

Dulwich Picture Gallery

73

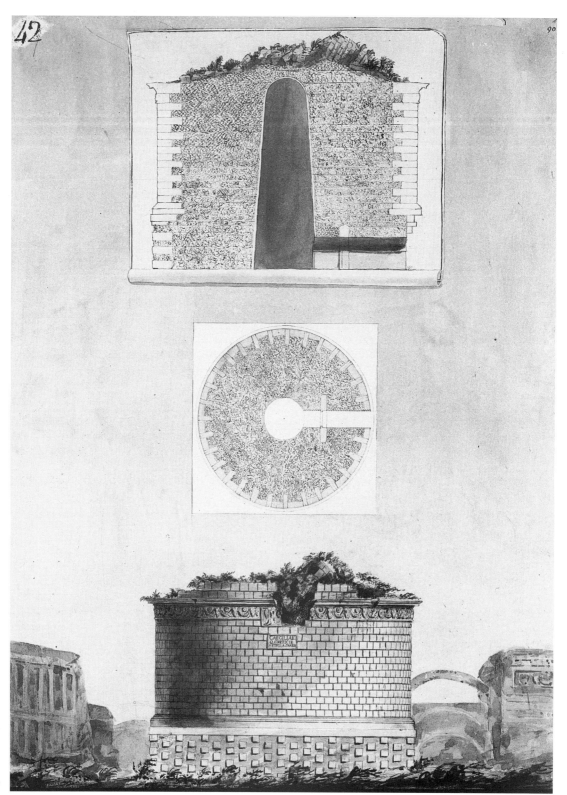

II.7

II & III

Soane's Lecture Illustrations

This exhibition includes several of the illustrations which Soane's pupils prepared under his direction for the lectures he delivered from 1809 in his capacity as Professor of Architecture at the Royal Academy. Over a thousand illustrations were made between 1806 and 1820, forming one of the most extraordinary and labour-intensive artistic productions of his office. The drawings are large objects, many of them as much as three or four feet long, each of which took at least a week's full-time work. Their production must have made life difficult in Soane's never very large drawing office. During the first three months of 1815, for example, all hands were devoted to the task of completing the illustrations for the new course of lectures. Soane had between four and six pupils a year who were busiest on the lecture illustrations between 1806 and 1815, at a time when the Napoleonic Wars reduced the number of ordinary architectural commissions. The principal pupils engaged in this work were Henry Parke, who was the ablest draughtsman of all, George Bailey, Edward Foxhall, Charles Tyrrell, George Basevi, James Adams, Robert Chantrell, Charles Papendiek, George Underwood and John Buxton.

Soane delivered courses of six lectures each, in February and March at the Royal Academy, then housed in Somerset House in the Strand. On lecture days, the relevant drawings were taken by carriage for the short distance from Lincoln's Inn Fields to the Royal Academy. His pupils helped hang them round the walls of the Great Room at the top of the Strand block where Soane lectured. Nothing like them had been seen before, so that tickets for the lectures were much sought after. In the large, not very well-lit, room, the drawings were not always clearly visible to the audience, but they were admired before and after the lectures, and were also sometimes available for inspection at 13 Lincoln's Inn Fields.

They fell into three principal groups. The most numerous were those based on engravings in architectural, topographical and antiquarian books in Soane's own extensive library, such as Fischer von Erlach, Piranesi, Wood, Stuart, Leroy, Choiseul-Gouffier, *Vitruvius Britannicus* and many others. To translate the black and white engravings into coloured views must have been a novel and exciting, though time-consuming, process. Then, there were views of buildings, mainly in London, which Soane's pupils were sent to draw on the spot. Finally, there were copies of Soane's designs for his own buildings and of designs by his contemporaries and immediate predecessors. In some drawings he combined on a single sheet buildings from different periods in a pioneering comparative approach for which he was indebted to hints in the writings of French architectural thinkers such as Leroy and Durand.

Soane's lecture illustrations constituted a public-spirited gesture for which he received no financial recompense, but which was the result of his Enlightenment commitment to civic virtue. It was in the same spirit that he eventually gave the Soane Museum itself to the public in what the French architect Jacques-Ignace Hittorff hailed in 1836 (in the *Annales de la Société Libre des Beaux-Arts*) as '*ce bel exemple de dévouement civique*'. Soane believed passionately in the value of architectural education, and the powerful coloured lecture illustrations are one of the principal fruits of that belief.

The lecture drawings all survive in the Soane Museum. They were copied by Soane's pupils, in a smaller format, from the 1810s to the 1830s, with most of the work latterly carried out by C. J. Richardson. Their place in the lectures is recorded in a set of nine manuscript volumes in the Museum, with the copies appropriately interleaved. A number of the drawings were used in more than one place in the lectures.

David Watkin

II ANCIENT BUILDINGS

II.1 *Treasury of Atreus, Mycenae – View of entrance*

The centre of Helladic civilisation (c.1200–2500 BC),
Mycenae was traditionally identified as the capital of
Homer's Agamemnon, and was known for the splendour of its culture. The so-called Treasury of Atreus was
a *tholos* tomb (i.e. with a circular domed chamber), con-
ceivably built for the presumed prototype of Agamemnon but certainly for a Mycenean ruler, and is dated to
c.1330 BC, at the height of Mycenean civilisation.
Though Mycenae was not systematically excavated until
the 1870s (by Schliemann) it was, as the modern visitors
in the view suggest, well known in Soane's day.

The Treasury was cited in Lecture VI as an example
of a building supposedly exhibiting early understanding of the construction of arches.

Pencil, ink and coloured washes (820 × 590)

SM 19/1/1

II.1

II.2 *The entrance to the Great Pyramid – View*

The Great Pyramid dates from the Third to the Sixth
Dynasties (2815–2294 BC). The pyramid as monument
to the dead was to exert a powerful influence on tomb
design in Roman times, an influence that was revived in
the late eighteenth and early nineteenth centuries with
the renewed interest in ancient Egypt, a taste whose
frivolous application Soane deplored.

This drawing illustrated Lecture VI, in a discussion of
the view, common at the time but questioned by Soane,
that the ancient Egyptians understood the construction
of arches.

Pencil and grey and brown washes (540 × 450)

SM 26/4/8

II.3 *Perspective of the Pyramids at Gezeh*

The pyramids at Gezeh were built during the Fourth
Dynasty (2700–2675 BC).

Soane greatly admired the pyramids, writing in his
Lecture I that they claimed 'no small degree of our
attention, and admiration. Their forms, although of the
most simple kind, produce the greatest variety of effect'.
The Great Pyramid especially aroused his enthusiasm
('this amazing Structure occupies a space of about
eleven acres, which is almost as large as the whole area
of Lincoln's Inn Fields') and he noted that 360,000 men

II.2

were said to have spent 70 years in erecting it. The pyramids were sufficient alone 'to immortalise the Sovereigns of Egypt, and to have proved the ardent and successful desire of the Egyptians to transmit their names to posterity'. So powerful was Egyptian building that 'neither time nor the convulsions of nature, nor the revolutions of Empires have destroyed, nor the power of merciless and exterpating [sic] conquerors removed them'. In Egyptian buildings could be found 'prodigious solidity and wonderful magnitude', but also a lack of true satisfaction for the spectator as a result of their 'uniformity and tiresome monotony'.

Pencil, pen and ink, and watercolour (440 × 690)

SM 27/3/2

II.4 *Mausoleum of Halicarnassus – Model*

The most famous of all mausolea and one of the Seven Wonders of the World was built by Artemisia, widow (and sister) of the eponymous Mausolus, ruler of Caria in Asia Minor, who died in 353 BC. The structure was of outstanding size and splendour, dominating the city of Halicarnassus, and was richly decorated with sculpture. It powerfully influenced the design of antique tombs. Destroyed in relatively modern times, it became the subject of much speculation and mental reconstruction by architects.

Soane referred to this mausoleum in Lecture I as the most impressive of all such buildings, recommending its reconstruction on paper as 'a fine subject to exercise the mind of the Artist' and commending Pliny the Elder's description of the building. In Lecture IV he quoted the building, on the evidence of Pliny's account, for its misuse of the pyramid, which was not applied 'in its simple and natural form' but placed above a peristyle. The builders 'set a bad example to the moderns'.

This model, like those of Mylassa and Palmyra, was made by François Fouquet, an internationally known model-maker working in Paris from the 1790s to the 1830s. Soane bought twenty Fouquet models in 1834. He regarded models as a particularly valuable form of communication, both in assessing the impact to be made by a projected building and, as he explained in Lecture XII, in conveying 'sensations and impressions of the highest kind' about the form and construction of buildings of the past.

Model, plaster-of-Paris (205 × 220 × 165)

SM MR37

II.5   *Monument at Mylassa – Model*

The monument at Mylassa, in Asia Minor, which survives in good condition, probably dates from the first or second century AD, and was inspired by Halicarnassus, though built on a much smaller scale. The monument was discussed as an example of 'very remote Antiquity' in Lectures I and VI, in architectural rather than associational terms, with particular reference to its detached pilasters and their anticipation of 'the regular arch'.

Model, plaster-of-Paris (205 × 160 × 160)

SM MR15

II.6   *Rome: Perspective of the Tomb of Caius Cestius*

This mausoleum on the outskirts of ancient Rome commemorates a praetor and tribune. Its pyramidal form reflects the continuing use of this shape in funerary buildings in Rome in accordance with the Roman enthusiasm for Egyptian culture, though Roman pyramids were relatively rare.

Soane discussed this tomb in Lecture IV, remarking on its smallness in comparison with the Egyptian pyramids and on recent archaeological work on the site; and again in Lecture XI where the application of the pyramid was cited as an example of the continuity of certain forms.

Pencil and watercolour (970 × 720)

SM 20/4/6

II.6

II.7   *Rome: Plan, elevation and section of the Tomb of Cecilia Metella, Via Appia*

This well-preserved circular tomb to a Roman aristocrat, wife and mother of consuls, dates from the first century BC. The circular mausoleum was a type frequently adopted by the Roman aristocracy, and this structure was much imitated.

This drawing was used by Soane in Lecture IV as an example 'of the desire of the Ancients to make the sepulchres of the dead of eternal durability'. It might have resisted Time 'but no construction can resist the power of Barbarism'. The tomb was cited again in Lecture IX as an example of a building altered long after its erection, a point young architects must be careful to recognise when assessing ancient buildings; and in Lecture X as one of the mausolea that pointed out 'most forcibly the departed grandeur of their former magnificence, and dazzling splendour', a monument 'of the mutability of all human expectations'.

Pencil, pen and ink, and watercolour (670 × 505)

SM 26/5/6

II.8

II.8 *Pompeii: Perspective of the Street of the Tombs*

As in many Roman cities, the custom at Pompeii was to line the main roads leading into the town with tombs, since the Romans wished their monuments to be seen by all. Soane expressed his admiration for this custom in Lecture IV. The theme re-emerged in Lecture XI (where this drawing was used), in which Soane contrasted the fineness of monuments in and around foreign cities with those in Britain, and especially London, stressing the role that had been played in the past and should be played in the present by architectural invention in creating funerary monuments.

Pencil, pen and ink, and watercolour (705 × 1250)

SM 20/4/7

II.9 *Monument at Palmyra – Model*

The state of Palmyra, an oasis situated in what is now Syria, survived until 274 AD when it was absorbed by the Roman Empire. Its characteristic funerary monument was the tower, up to six storeys high with burial places on each level, and probably used for religious ritual. Palmyra was frequently discussed in Soane's lectures,

with various of its temples illustrated. Through these mighty ruins it was possible, Soane suggested in Lecture X, to gain an impression of the character of ancient Byzantium.

Model, plaster-of-Paris (340 × 180 × 180)

SM MR34

Bernard de Montfaucon (1653–1741)

II.10 *L'Antiquité Expliquée et Représentée en Figures. Tôme Cinquième: Les Funerailles, Les Lampes, Les Supplices &c.*

This publication, much used by architects, was closely studied by Soane who annotated his copy. It brought together engravings from various sources, to illustrate the most important classical buildings and artefacts. Many of the lecture drawings derived from engravings in these volumes. The influence on Soane's tomb designs was considerable, Miss Johnston's tomb, for example, being inspired by Montfaucon's print of the tomb of Cecilia Metella.

Folio, Paris 1719, vol. V

Sir John Soane's Museum

III.1

III CONTEMPORARY CEMETERIES

III.1 *Castle Howard, Yorkshire – Elevation of the Mausoleum*

The mausoleum designed by Nicholas Hawksmoor from 1729 onwards for the third Earl of Carlisle, the builder of Castle Howard, was the first monumental free-standing tomb built since Antiquity, and also notable for being erected in open country rather than on sacred ground. It was intended both as a feature of the park and as a statement of family pride, conceived in a secular rather than religious spirit. The Castle Howard mausoleum was much visited and its close resemblance to classical tombs inspired other private mausolea in Britain. Though acknowledged by Soane as the work of Hawksmoor (whom he considered to be Vanbrugh's pupil), the building was illustrated (with this drawing) in Lecture V as an indication that Sir John Vanbrugh, an architect whom Soane admired with reservations over his lack of classical correctness, 'occasionally felt the force of the Simplicity of the Ancients.'

Pen and ink, and grey and coloured washes (660 × 505)

SM 73/3/1

III.2

James Wyatt RA (1746–1813)

III.2 *Cobham Hall, Kent – Elevation of the Mausoleum*

Signed and dated 1782

Pen and ink, grey and coloured washes (520 × 365)

SM 47/10/20

James Wyatt

III.3 *Cobham Hall, Kent – Section of the Mausoleum*

Signed and dated 1782

These two drawings were exhibited at the Royal Academy in 1783, the year of Wyatt's election as Academician.

The mausoleum built according to the will of the third Earl of Darnley was executed in 1783–4 by James Wyatt, architect of some of the most distinguished late eighteenth-century monuments in England. It has for

80

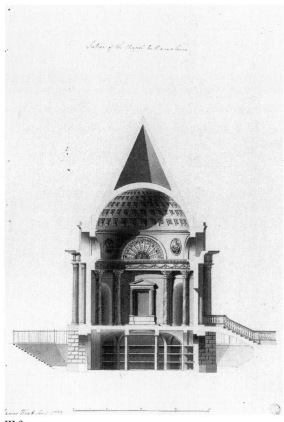

III.3

III.4

(faithful, apart from the omission of a few minor figures) of the Clérisseau original, also in the collection, and was used to illustrate Lecture XI. Soane intended it to illustrate the decoration by the Ancients of their mausolea with 'various kinds of grotesque forms', as well as the decoration applied to sarcophagi, but he stressed that such ornament was applied not arbitrarily but with a specific purpose.

Pencil, pen and brown ink, and coloured washes (505 × 635)

SM 26/5/12

many disgraceful years been decaying in spite of efforts at preservation.

In Lecture IV Soane described the Cobham mausoleum as 'magnificent' but regretted that, inspired by bad classical precedent, its Doric order was surmounted by a pyramid, following the instructions of the patron (which did not justify this solecism). It seems probable that he used these drawings as illustrations.

Pen and ink, grey and coloured washes (515 × 360)

SM 47/10/21

After Charles-Louis Clérisseau

III.4 *Perspective of a sepulchral chamber, with a Body being carried in*

Between 1797 and 1806 Soane bought twenty drawings by Charles-Louis Clérisseau (1721–1820), a French architect and draughtsman who spent much of his career in Rome and exerted a strong influence on Robert Adam. This drawing is a copy by Soane's office

Joseph Bonomi RA (1739-1808)

III.5 *Mausoleum at Blickling Hall, Norfolk*

This pyramidal mausoleum was erected to the designs of Bonomi, a notably correct neoclassical architect, in the park at Blickling in memory of the second Earl of Buckinghamshire in 1796–7. Though Soane does not refer to it in his lectures, it represents the type of grand aristocratic monument, in a pure style, which he never had the opportunity to design himself.

It is worth noting that the nephew of the Earl of Buckinghamshire for whom this mausoleum was built was a close acquaintance of Francis Bourgeois and advised him on the fate of his collection.

Pen and pink, yellow and blue washes (486 × 660)

Royal Architectural Library of Drawings Collection, RIBA

III.6

III.6 *Père Lachaise – General View*

Pencil and watercolour (645 × 1265)

SM 22/6/1

III.7 *Père Lachaise – General View*

The cemetery of Père Lachaise was laid out by the city of Paris to the designs of Alexandre-Théodore Brongniart from 1804 onwards, in response to the pressing need for additional burial space in the French capital. It has been described by Howard Colvin as the archetype of the new picturesque cemetery created outside the traditional churchyard. The cemetery was laid out as a picturesque garden on the slope of a hill. From an early date it was regarded as a place suitable for contemplation by the Romantically-inclined visitor, whose mood of delightful melancholy would be enhanced by such spectacles as the reconstructed tomb of Héloïse and Abelard, brought to Père Lachaise in 1817 from the Musée des Monuments Français (itself conceived in a very similar spirit) specifically with such visitors in mind. The cemetery was to inspire many comparable sites, with Kensal Green Cemetery in London as one of the earliest examples.

Soane was greatly struck by Père Lachaise on his visit to Paris in 1819, and arranged for Henry Parke to draw it on 9 September. His comment in a note on Lecture IV, in which funerary buildings are discussed at length, may be applied to the view in III.6: 'How wonderfully the towns of magnificent buildings in honour of the dead inspire the soul and prepare the mind for those grand effects produced by the steeples, towers, spires, and domes of great cities, when viewed at a distance'. In Lecture X he dwelt on the affective relationship between landscaped gardens and ruins, notably the ruins of monuments: the realisation of such a landscape in this cemetery was clearly congenial to him.

Pencil and watercolour (715 × 1180)

SM 22/6/2

IV

Tomb for Miss Elizabeth Johnston, 1784

IV.2

St Mary Abbot's Churchyard, Kensington

Sir John Soane's Museum: a contract design and 2 record drawings

The tomb of Miss Johnston was commissioned by her lover and bigamous husband, Charles Coote, Earl of Bellamont (1738–1800). Immortalised in one of Sir Joshua Reynolds' most alluring full-length portraits in the robes of the Order of the Bath (fig. 1), he allowed his early military prowess to be overwhelmed by his passionate interest in women, which gained him the epithet of 'the Hibernian Seducer'. He was particularly drawn to young and innocent women, untouched by other men.

It was no doubt these qualities that he found attractive in Elizabeth Johnston (d.1784), the daughter of a London tradesman. The history of their involvement, long forgotten, has recently been pieced together, largely from (his) family traditions. According to these sources, the Earl married her bigamously, their son being born in 1781 or 1782. Lord Bellamont looked after his numerous illegitimate children well, and this child, Charles Coote, was left Bellamont Forest, the elegant Palladian family house in Co. Cavan.

The tomb cost the Earl £234.1.8d., including Soane's fee of £21.0.0d., and was carved by John Hinchcliff senior.

The source for Soane's design – common to the

Claude Bosanquet and Bridport monuments – was the sarcophagus of Cecilia Metella as illustrated in Montfaucon: the tomb might also be seen as a neoclassical reordering of the traditional tomb-chest. The use of grooving in an elongated S-shape, known as strigillation, was a motif that was to recur in Soane's tombs and had a specifically funerary association, being related to the use of the *strigillus*, the curved blade with which embalming oil was scraped from a dead body.

LITERATURE: `Michael Hall, 'Mending Monuments', *Country Life*, 14 June 1990, pp. 302–3; Michael Hall, 'Contemplating Paradise', *Country Life*, 5 January 1995, pp. 38–9

IV.1   *Contract design: Elevation of the flank, section through tomb and plinth and detail of lid moulding, with sketches for the base of the tomb in Soane's hand.*

This drawing is one of those relating to the contract made between Soane and the mason Hinchcliff on 24 July 1784, and is signed by both parties.

Pen and pink wash (490 × 295)

SM 63/6/19

IV.2   *Final design: perspective in a landscape setting*

Signed and dated July 20 1784

Pencil, pen and ink, and wash (250 × 389)

SM Vol. 12 folio 15

John Russell RA (1745–1806)
IV.3   *Miss Elizabeth Johnston and her son*

Pastel (600 × 445)

Private collection

John Russell
IV.4   *Charles Coote, Earl of Bellamont*

Pastel (600 × 445)

Private collection

Above: IV.3. Below: Fig. 1 Sir Joshua Reynolds, *Charles Coote, Earl of Bellamont* (National Gallery of Ireland, Dublin)

V

Evelyn Column, 1785

Memorial to Mr and Mrs Evelyn, at Felbridge Place, Surrey; moved to Lemmington Hall, Northumberland, 1927

Sir John Soane's Museum: Preliminary and final designs (2), working drawing and perspective.

This 50-foot-high column was erected in memory of his *'benignissimi parentes'* (as the inscription puts it), the Surrey landowners Edward and Julia Evelyn, by James Evelyn, a philanthropically-minded individual responsible for founding both Felbridge School and the Beef and Faggot Charities. The column was a type of structure which, as Soane remarked in Lecture IV, was erected in ancient times 'to record the actions of great men'. Soane at first proposed an Ionic column and an obelisk on a circular plinth. The filial dedication on the plinth is followed by the words of Addison's *Hymn of Gratitude*. Soane here used for the first time symbolism that was to recur in his funerary designs: the Roman altar (decorated with carved flames, which may symbolise the offerings made by later generations in memory of the dead), and the serpent devouring its tail, an Egyptian symbol of eternity.

The property was carved up for building plots in 1927 and the column was removed by Mr Stephen Aitchison to his Northumberland estate.

V.1   *Perspective view*

This view is by the same artist as VII.1, showing the Colne Engaine column of 1791, and was probably painted some years after the Evelyn column was erected. The artist did not visit the site but worked from an elevation in the Soane office (SM 65/7/3).

Pen and ink and coloured washes (510 × 360)

SM 65/3/6

V.1

VI.2

VI

Monument to Claude Bosanquet, 1786

St Stephen's Church, Coleman Street, London;
destroyed by bombing, 1940

Sir John Soane's Museum: 2 drawings

Soane became acquainted with the Huguenot
banking family of the Bosanquets when he met
Richard Bosanquet, whose bank had recently
failed, in Naples in 1778. He formed a long association with the family.

Claude Bosanquet (1707–86) was a successful
merchant dealing prosperously with the East
(especially in the traditionally Huguenot trade of
cloth), who supported Huguenot causes, including the French Hospital. He was the bachelor
uncle of Richard and Samuel Bosanquet. He
bequeathed £10,000 to Samuel who commissioned this monument and who was to have his
own monument designed by Soane. In his first
design for a wall monument, Soane had to apply
his developing ornamental vocabulary in low
relief. Serpents are used both in the urn handles
and in the tympanum of the pediment.

VI. 1   *Preliminary design*

Soane copied this drawing in 1816 when working on the
Bridport monument (XII).

Pen and watercolour (385 × 230)

SM 63/6/16

VI.2   *Final design*

This is an extremely fine drawing, in Soane's own hand,
showing the front and side elevations, the plan and a
vertical section; the artist has used light and shadow to
create a *trompe l'oeil* effect of depth, and has contrasted
the varying surfaces of the marbles.

Pen and watercolour (580 × 445)

SM 63/6/21

VI.1

87

VII

Colne Park Column, 1790

For Michael Hills, at Colne Park, Colne Engaine, Essex

Sir John Soane's Museum: 1 drawing

Michael Hills (c.1742–89) was a wealthy landowner and a collector of curiosities, who in 1775 built himself a large house at Colne Park in north Essex, where he laid out the grounds, according to his obituary in the *Gentlemen's Magazine*, 'with true taste and judgement'. He left the bulk of his property to a 22-year-old friend, Philip Astle, on condition that the latter adopt his surname. Philip 'Hills' erected the column in honour of his benefactor in a field in full view of the mansion. Designs were sent to the patron in June 1790, and it was completed in September 1791. The column stands 70 foot high and was originally surmounted by a copper cinerary urn, topped with a pineapple, rather than the caduceus shown in this drawing. It cost £1,165.

The column has suffered various vicissitudes including being used for target practice, and the urn blew off in 1987. It was restored by the Essex Heritage Trust with help from the Soane Monuments Trust in 1991.

VII.1   *Perspective view of column*

In the original design, the Ionic capital is surmounted by two snakes twisting round a column in the form of a caduceus, surmounted by a pineapple. This scheme was abandoned in favour of an urn.

Pencil, pen and ink, and coloured washes (510 × 360)

SM 65/3/5

VII.1

VIII

Obelisk to Edward Simeon, 1804

Market Place, Reading, Berkshire

Sir John Soane's Museum: 9 drawings, including site plans, views, elevations and details

Edward Simeon (c.1755–1812), native of Reading, City merchant and Director of the Bank of England, offered in 1804 to build an obelisk-lampstand in Reading market place, with an endowment for its market lamps to be lit in perpetuity, 'as a mark of affection to his native Town' as the inscription put it. Simeon's brother had recently lost his Parliamentary seat in Reading and the lamp post was interpreted by some as a political statement, being ridiculed by the *Reading Mercury* (September 1804) as 'a paltry gewgaw thing without use or name'.

In July Soane spent three days in Reading supervising construction. His obelisk had the character of a memorial, with the base as a Roman sacrificial altar, and the fasces acknowledging the authority of Reading Corporation. The original square plan of the memorial was replaced by a triangular one, perhaps to suit the shape of the market place. It survives, but its present setting, hemmed in by traffic controls and public lavatories, scarcely recalls the Via Appia. Current proposals, if implemented, may improve the situation.

VIII.1

VIII.1 *Preliminary design: perspective*

Pencil, pen and ink, and coloured washes (465 × 290)

SM 65/3/10

VIII.2 *Model of design as executed*

Model, wood (760 × 200 × 180)

SM MR38

LITERATURE: Alan Windsor, 'The Simeon Monument in Reading by Sir John Soane' in *English Architecture Public and Private: Essays for Kerry Downes*, ed. John Bold and Edward Chaney, London 1993

IX

Monument to Samuel Bosanquet, 1806

St Mary's Church, Leyton

Sir John Soane's Museum: 26 drawings including preliminary designs, a working drawing and a watercolour view of the tomb

Samuel Bosanquet (1744–1806) was an active director of the Bank of England, serving as Governor 1791–3. During the invasion scare of 1804 plans were made to despatch the records, ledgers and note-printing presses of the Bank for safekeeping to his Monmouthshire home, Dingestow Court. Soane, who held the position of quartermaster in the recently-formed Bank of England Volunteers, was responsible for making these arrangements.

Soane had carried out alterations to Bosanquet's country house, Forest House at Leyton, then a pleasant village to the east of London. On Bosanquet's death in July 1806, the architect designed his monument, visiting the site on 1 August and determining to site the tomb so that it formed a focal point in the vista down the nave of the church. This was Soane's most ambitious monument, apart from the family tomb and the Bourgeois mausoleum. It is seen towards the foreground of Gandy's *A Selection of Buildings erected from the designs of J. Soane, Esq., RA, between 1780 and 1815.*

The scheme went through a number of stages but the essential ideas remained the same throughout. The first two designs were sent to Bosanquet's widow as watercolour perspectives on 13 August. The next day, Soane added the central feature of a pendentive dome, placed on a pedestal and surmounted by an urn. This innovative feature anticipated the canopy of his wife's monument. Three models were made, of which IX.6 corresponds to the executed design, but without the plinth.

The tomb cost £300, with some excess expenditure for the railings and for carving the inscrip-

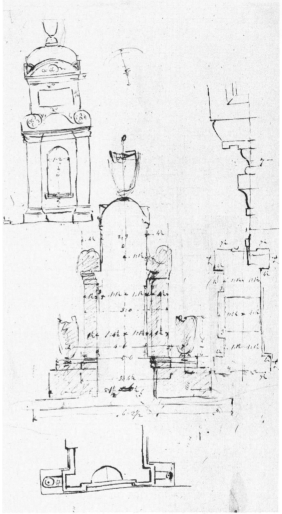

IX.1

tion. As was not unusual with memorials to his friends, Soane charged no commission and paid for a proportion of the excess over estimate.

The tomb was demolished around 1958, following vandalism. It had been thought that no trace survived but Ptolemy Dean, visiting in 1994, discovered the base to be intact.

IX.1 *Sketches in Soane's hand of the end elevation, vertical section, and plan; a section of the cornice moulding is sketched on a larger scale*

This drawing is the verso of a sheet dated 5 September 1806, showing an elevation in pen and grey wash.

Brown ink (550 × 320)

SM 63/6/25 verso

IX.2 *Perspective view of the monument as erected, shown in a landscape setting, with coat-of-arms and inscription illustrated*

The drawing is inscribed by George Bailey and dated 'May 1808'. It was executed by Adams, one of Soane's pupils, over a period of four days in the year after the monument's erection.

Pen and ink, and watercolour (560 × 340)

SM 63/6/48

Charles Turner RA (1773–1857) after George Romney (1734–1802)

IX.3 *Samuel Bosanquet*

The portrait was painted by Romney in 1792 and the mezzotint was published by Colnaghi, 2 December 1806. A version was hung by Soane in his Breakfast Room.

Mezzotint (506 × 354)

The Governor and Company of the Bank of England

IX.4 *List of Governors and Directors of the Bank of England, 1694–1961*

This volume was kept by the Secretary of the Bank as a record of the composition of the Court of Directors, the governing body of the Bank of England.

MS volume (open 340 × 220)

The Governor and Company of the Bank of England

IX.5, 6, 7

IX.5 *Model for the Tomb of Samuel Bosanquet*

Model, plaster-of-Paris (400 × 180 × 280)

SM MR33

IX.6 *Model for the Tomb of Samuel Bosanquet*

Model, plaster-of-Paris (410 × 165 × 275)

SM MP217

IX.7 *Model for the Tomb of Samuel Bosanquet*

Model, plaster-of-Paris (450 × 150 × 240)

SM MP222

X

Desenfans/Bourgeois Mausolea, 1807/1811

Mausoleum at Charlotte(now Hallam) Street, London for Noel Desenfans (1807); and mausoleum at Dulwich Picture Gallery for Mr and Mrs Desenfans and Sir Francis Bourgeois RA (1811–13)

Sir John Soane's Museum: 83 drawings

The French-born art-dealer Noel Desenfans (1745–1807) and the Swiss-born painter Sir Francis Bourgeois (1756–1811), are buried with Mrs Margaret Desenfans at Dulwich Picture Gallery, where the collection which they assembled for the King of Poland but were never able to deliver to him, survives. Bourgeois was a close friend of Soane, and his ally in various Royal Academy battles; several works by the artist, including his self-portrait, hang in the Soane Museum. It was Bourgeois' wish that Soane should design the necessary alterations when he left his collection of pictures to Dulwich College as the basis for what was intended to be the first National Gallery. The architect's willingness to execute the work without charge illustrates the tenderness with which he regarded this commission.

For Desenfans and Bourgeois, art provided a means of entering society during life and of achieving immortality after death. Typically, the latter gave instructions that their mausoleum at Dulwich should be built 'as far as possible of marble', without providing the financial resources to construct even a much more modest structure.

The first tomb for Desenfans was built in the backyard of the house which he, his wife and Bourgeois shared in Charlotte (now Hallam) Street, off Portland Place. Soane produced the first design for this 'Private Chapel' (as Bourgeois described it in his will, its chaplain being one of the Fellows of Dulwich College) on 15 August 1807 (X.1). The rectangular chamber originally proposed was succeeded by a domed circular 'chapel' leading into the burial chamber which from the first was planned to contain three tombs. This scheme was executed and Desenfans was buried there. The interior of the Charlotte Street tomb was very close to the Dulwich mausoleum, but the exigencies of the site meant that no exterior elevations were created.

In spite of Bourgeois' efforts, permission was not given for the collection and mausoleum to remain at Charlotte Street. In his last days of life, Bourgeois instead determined on Dulwich College as recipient for his collection, planning that the pictures would be shown in the College's existing small gallery. His executors were instructed to ensure that the friends' remains should be 'deposited in the Chapel at Dulwich College ... in a Tomb or Sarcophagus'.

Bourgeois died on 7 January 1811 and Soane made his first site visit the following day. The complex planning and building history of the Gallery, considerable evidence for which survives in Sir John Soane's Museum, has been discussed elsewhere (see Mellinghoff 1983, Waterfield 1986). In brief, Bourgeois's plan to use the old buildings of the College for these new purposes were soon seen to be impractical, and in May 1811 the architect submitted five designs for the erection of a new quadrangle, with the gallery occupying the whole of one side. Not until 12 July was a new scheme approved: broadly speaking, the one erected. Work started in October 1811 and the exterior was completed by September 1812. As a result of financial and engineering difficulties, progress then became slow, and Soane's original intentions were compromised: for example, his plan for a major central axis was abandoned in favour of a temporary entrance at the south end. The pictures were not moved to Dulwich until September 1814 and the bodies followed in March 1815, Bourgeois having been temporarily accommodated at Charlotte Street. The Gallery opened to visitors in 1817.

The Gallery was damaged by a bomb in 1944, which destroyed the north and east sides of the mausoleum. Restoration was completed in 1952, with the building reconstructed as far aspossible.

X.5

X.1 *Proposal for interior of mausoleum at 38 Charlotte Street, London*

In an early proposal, the mausoleum was shown as a rectangular chamber, with Doric columns supporting a groin vault and vaguely classical reliefs. The lighting from lunettes persisted in later schemes, but this initial idea was otherwise far from the solution reached.

Pen and ink with coloured wash (253 × 230)

Trustees of the Victoria and Albert Museum, London

X.2 *Desenfans mausoleum, 38 Charlotte Street, London*

Signed and dated 1807, and inscribed TO THE MEMORY OF NOEL DESENFANS ESQR.; HIS. SALTEM. ACCUMULEM. DONIS. ET. FUNGAE. INANIMUNERE.

X.2

The Charlotte Street mausoleum was entered from an angle on account of the restrictions of the site, and this aspect is reflected in the viewpoint of the drawing. Like the view of the Dulwich mausoleum, the drawing is notable for the contrast between the tomb chamber, strongly lit from above, and the darkness of the ante-chamber, in which a group of figures dressed in mourning fulfil the vital role (discussed by Roger Bowdler) of the living contemplating the dead. The central tomb (very similar to the Ionic aedicule tomb built for Lord Bridport), and the inscription above the arch, are dedicated to Noel Desenfans, who was to be supplanted in this position of prominence by Bourgeois in the Dulwich mausoleum, but the existence of the two subsidiary tombs underlines Bourgeois' hope that this mausoleum would ultimately contain the bodies of all three friends. The theatrical quality of this scheme is reinforced by the use of three steps between the ante-chamber and the tomb-chamber, echoing the three steps planned for the external doors at Dulwich – though in both cases the present building has two steps only. The other striking difference between this and the Dulwich design is the circular containing wall, as compared to the rectangular space at Dulwich: in both this and the drawing of Dulwich the wall is shown as painted to imitate ashlar, suggesting that such was Soane's original intention in contrast to the plain paint that has

existed for many years.

On this Charlotte Street scheme the articulation of the decoration is considerably richer than that in the executed structure, notably in the linear emphasis of the circular floor and the illusionistic fluting around the ceiling, though it is not clear that these features were carried out. Another aspect emerging from this drawing is the importance of the narrow arches between the two chambers, which were intended to allow a picturesque glimpse from ante-chamber to tomb-chamber. Although at Dulwich three pairs of lateral arches do exist, the third being blank, the effect is diminished by the raising of the base and the reduction of the tombs to a lower level. The Charlotte Street mausoleum also differed from Dulwich in the organisation of the ceiling above the tombs: in the earlier version a vaulted ceiling sprang from the lower entablature.

An intriguing aspect of this and X.6 is the manipulation of the ceiling, which is shown out of perspective, an idea influenced by contemporary French theoreticians. The Piranesian candelabra seem to have been intended by Soane to introduce a sense of balance to an irregular space.

Pencil, pen and ink, and watercolour (650 × 645)

SM 15/2/1

X.3

X.4

X.3 *Perspective of exterior of mausoleum, Dulwich Picture Gallery*

This drawing, probably by Gandy, conveys the essential character of the building but with considerable embellishment of detail. These adornments should be interpreted as representing the artist's fancy rather than, necessarily, the architect's intention: though the spirit of the drawing, with the mausoleum entirely in Portland stone rather than brick, is close to the patron's original ambitions. The artist has conveyed the role of the mausoleum as the centrepiece of the building, brilliantly lit in contrast to the dark gallery and almshouses behind, and with its lantern boldly elongated. Structurally the drawing differs from the executed building: for example in the rectangular plinth with rounded corners on which the mausoleum stands, and in the windows for the almshouses, which exhibit the curious neo-Jacobean design with which Soane originally attempted to evoke the character of old Dulwich College next door.

Pen and ink and bodycolour (730 × 1275)

SM 15/2/3

96

X.4 *Perspective of mausoleum, Dulwich Picture Gallery*

This relatively clumsy drawing again emphasises Soane's interest in treating the mausoleum almost as a distinct building: here the relation between mausoleum and almshouses is so indistinct as to suggest that the former is a free-standing structure. The impression is strengthened by the depiction of the rear building as a one-storey structure, as contemplated at an early stage of the planning. Though Soane's ideas for the building are already close to those finally executed, he here experiments with the introduction, at least in the space actually occupied by the central door, of a columbarium with a Roman altar in front of it.

Pencil, pen and ink and watercolour (870 × 800)

SM 15/2/7

X.5 *Perspective of mausoleum, Dulwich Picture Gallery*

This drawing, one of many progress drawings made by Soane's pupils, is inscribed 'May 21st 1812'. George Basevi and R. D. Chantrell are recorded as drawing at Dulwich on that day as well as several days earlier. The mausoleum is shown without the glass installed in the lantern, and with the doors or altars not yet in place.

Pencil, pen and ink and bodycolour (910 × 655)

SM 15/2/5

X.6 *Interior perspective of mausoleum, Dulwich Picture Gallery*

This ambitious drawing was probably intended for exhibition at the Royal Academy.

Like X.2, this drawing represents the essentials of the executed building but considerably elaborates on the details. The figures discussing the plan emphasise by their gestures the essential character of the structure, the tomb-chamber contrasted with the dark ante-room. In the latter space, the principal distinction between the drawing and the executed building lies in the richness of the decoration, with the fluted columns, the 'ashlared' walls and the patterned floor, all features contributing to the painterly quality of the interior but in fact omitted, presumably for reasons of economy. The tomb-chamber differs more radically from the executed building. The lunette shown here recalls the segmental wall above the tombs in the Charlotte Street mau-

X.6

soleum, later developed by Soane at Dulwich into rectangular clerestories, while the tombs are quite unlike the austere forms actually built. Here the tomb-chest supported on feet and a base is flanked by two tombs at the side which recall the sarcophagus of Cecilia Metella, used by Soane in his design for Miss Johnston. It is not clear when he developed the very plain forms, in *faux-porphyry*, which were eventually created, though the similarity of the base of the central tomb to the built design leads one to suppose that he always envisaged a more elaborate scheme, and that what was actually constructed was, so to speak, a double-base.

Pen and ink, and bodycolour (800 × 800)

SM F91

James Northcote RA (1746–1831)
X.7 *Noel Desenfans*

Oil (oval 733 × 609)

Dulwich Picture Gallery

Sir William Beechey RA (1753-1839)
X.8 *Sir Francis Bourgeois*

Oil (765 × 641)

Dulwich Picture Gallery

XI

Wall Tablet to Abraham Newland, 1808

Southwark Cathedral, London

Sir John Soane's Museum: 2 drawings

Abraham Newland (1730–1807) died on 21 November 1807, at 38 Highbury Place, leaving a considerable part of his £200,000 fortune to his housekeeper, Mrs Cornthwaite, who commissioned this tablet in the south choir of what was then St Saviour's, Southwark.

Newland, a miller's son whose life was described as 'less marked by enterprise than by enduring patience and plodding perseverance', joined the Bank as an eighteen-year-old clerk. As Chief Cashier from 1782, he slept on site for the last 25 years of his career, making a daily excursion to Highbury Place for tea and a stroll. The tomb inscription records that he had for 30 years *sedulously applied / the powers of an unusually energetic mind / to the various and important duties of / the Office of CHIEF CASHIER…'*.

Shortly before his death Newland wrote his own epitaph:

'Beneath this stone old ABRAHAM lies;
Nobody laughs, and nobody cries,
Where he is gone, and how he fares,
No one knows, and no one cares.'

Nonetheless, as reported in *Bell's Weekly Messenger*, the funeral was impressive. When the procession passed the Bank on the way from Highbury to St Saviour's, it consisted of 'Two Bank porters; ten persons in deep mourning on horseback; a plume of feathers; the hearse, containing the body; six mourning coaches; his private carriage; and a number of gentlemen's carriages. The deceased was driven by his own coachman. On the body passing the back part of the Royal Exchange, there was a momentary suspension of all business; every one stood to contemplate the remains of this worthy and respectable man.'

For the monument, Soane chose the form of a

Grecian stele, first re-used by Thomas Banks in church memorials of around 1790 in contrast to the earlier pedimented tablet. The tablet widens towards the base and is surmounted by a triangular pediment and two anthemion acroteria. A serpent is entwined in the tympanum. The quality of execution of this modest memorial, suited to the social position of its subject, is exceptionally high.

XI.1 *Design and working drawing for a monumental wall tablet to the memory of Mr Abraham Newland*

Soane has added to a version of a presentation drawing, details including a vertical section, measurements and annotations about materials. It is identified in George Bailey's hand, with working annotations including 'All in one piece of best statuary marble; Black marble'; and a rough estimate totalling £76. It is dated 7 May 1808 in Soane's hand.

Pen and wash on a folded sheet of paper (340 × 545)

SM 63/6/10

John Dye Collier

XI.2 *The Life of Abraham Newland, Esq., late Principal Cashier at the Bank of England; with Some Account of that Great National Establishment*

This exceptionally unexciting work depicts a life of virtue and devotion to duty: as the writer warns, it contains no 'deep involutions of distress powerfully to excite the sensibility of the reader' but the reader may gain some hints on 'how to become happy'. Of Newland, Collier says, 'No human being was his enemy, he injured no one, he conferred benefits on all with whom he was connected, he lived in credit and usefulness, and he died in peace.'

Octavo, London 1808

The Governor and Company of the Bank of England

Samuel Drummond ARA (1765–1844)

XI.3 *Abraham Newland,* 1802

Newland, shown holding a five pound note, was described by his biographer as 'of pleasing features, and a cheerful aspect'. The engraving was used as the frontispiece of Newland's life, and was published in *The European Magazine* in 1803. The Bank of England also owns a portrait of Newland by Romney painted in 1794–5.

Oil (1088 × 885)

The Governor and Company of the Bank of England

Charles Dibdin (1745–1814)

XI.4 *Abraham Newland*

The song 'As sung by Mr. Davis with universal Applause at Sadlers Wells' includes a verse which illustrates how well known the name of Newland was:

> *For fashion or arts, should you seek foreign parts,*
> *It matters not wherever you land,*
> *Jew Christian or Greek, the same language they speak*
> *That's the language of Abraham Newland*
> *Oh Abraham Newland*
> *Tho' compliments cramm'd you may die and be d–'d*
> *If you hav'n't an Abraham Newland.*

Printed songsheet (340 × 220)

The Governor and Company of the Bank of England

XI.3

XI. 5 *Bank notes or 'Newlands'*

(a) Denomination of £1,000 dated 12 April 1793
(b) Denomination of £1 dated 16 April 1798
(c) Denomination of £5 dated 3 November 1807

The earliest notes issued by the Bank of England were receipts for cash, that is to say coin, deposits. Consequently they were made payable to the depositor and the words 'or bearer' added to allow them to circulate. Despite the introduction of denominations – the £10 in 1759, £5 in 1793 and £1 and £2 in 1797 – notes could not, for legal reasons, be made payable as they are today simply 'to bearer'. To overcome this obstacle the name of the Chief Cashier was inserted in the payee clause from 1782 (until 1855) and Abraham Newland's name therefore appeared on the Bank's notes for 25 years. The public became so familiar with the name that the popular name for Bank of England notes was 'Newlands'.

The Governor and Company of the Bank of England

XII

Monument to Philippe Jacques de Loutherbourg RA, 1812

Sketches of designs for a Monumental Tomb for P.J. DeLoutherbourg Esqr R.a

Here I fix my Choice Mrs. de Loutherbourg

XII.1

Churchyard of St Nicholas' Church, Chiswick

Sir John Soane's Museum: 5 drawings including preliminary designs and working drawings.

De Loutherbourg (1740–1812) was born in Strasbourg. After early success as a painter in Paris, he left France for London in 1771. He was soon employed by David Garrick as a scene-painter, and retained an interest in introducing theatrical effects into landscape throughout his career, an interest which stimulated his invention of the *Eidophusikon*, a moving peepshow lit from behind. He specialised in decorative landscapes and scenes of adventure.

The artist became an intimate of many leading London artists and architects, and was elected Academician in 1781. Among his friends were

Noel Desenfans and Sir Francis Bourgeois, whose inclusion of two de Loutherbourgs in their bequest to Dulwich College in 1811 marked a rare acknowledgement of a contemporary artist, and the Soanes.

De Loutherbourg died on 11 March 1812. Soane presented three options to his widow, based on three designs drawn up six years before for the Samuel Bosanquet monument and reproduced without variation (XII.1). By late April Mrs de Loutherbourg had selected the least ambitious scheme. Later drawings show four stages in the refinement of the design, in particular through the recession of the end panels and the architraves of the corner piers. George Basevi prepared the working drawings in May and June 1812 (XII.2). The tomb was executed by Thomas Grundy, the mason who worked regularly for

100

Soane at the Bank of England from 1807, and who also executed the Desenfans sarcophagus of 1807, the Soane family tomb, and the Storace and Bridport monuments.

The design gave great satisfaction. In October 1812 Mrs de Loutherbourg wrote to Soane: 'For taste, elegance, and simplicity of design, nothing could have surpast it, or have met my ideas more fully. My friends are all highly pleased with it. Mr Grundy I think has done his work extremely well.'

Following a period of neglect, the tomb was restored in 1926, and again in recent years by the Chiswick Society.

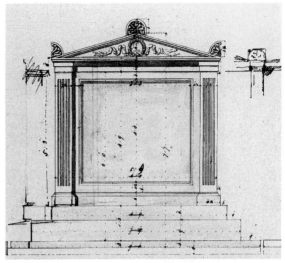

XII.2 (detail)

XII.1 *Three perspectives showing variant designs, on a sheet which can be folded to display the designs individually*

This drawing was sent to Mrs de Loutherbourg for her decision: beneath the third drawing she wrote 'Here I fix my choice'. It is dated 23 April 1812.

Pencil, pen and coloured wash (285 × 470)

SM 63/6/5

XII.2 *Plan, elevations, and section of tomb, with variant sketches for acroteria added in pen, in Soane's hand*

The drawing is dated' May 27th 1812'.

Pen, with pink and grey wash, and proposed alterations in brown ink (470 × 585)

SM 63/6/9

Thomas Gainsborough, RA (1727–88)

XII.3 *Philippe Jacques de Loutherbourg*

XII.3

Gainsborough and de Loutherbourg, who were close friends, painted one another in 1778. The portrait of Gainsborough is at the Yale Center for British Art, New Haven.

Oil (765 × 632)

Dulwich Picture Gallery

XIII.4

XIII

Monument to Alexander Hood, First Viscount Bridport, 1814

Church of St Thomas, Cricket St Thomas, Somerset

Sir John Soane's Museum: 23 preliminary designs, the final design and a working drawing for a wall monument in the chancel to Lord Bridport.

Alexander Hood (1727–1814) came from a leading naval family. At the age of thirteen he enlisted in the Navy with his elder brother Samuel, who also became an admiral and a viscount, and was described by Nelson as 'the best officer ... that England has to boast of'. By 1794 Alexander was second-in-command of the Channel Fleet, of which he was effectively in command from 1797 to 1800. He gained a solid reputation, though he was never popularly regarded as a heroic figure. He became baron in 1796 and viscount in 1801.

The Bridports and the Soanes were on very friendly terms. Soane carried out several commissions at Cricket Lodge, the family's (surviving) house in Somerset, and acted as agent for the Bridports' London property. Mrs Soane's Note Books record frequent excursions with Lady Bridport when the latter visited London.

The Admiral's monument does not resemble the patriotic monuments erected in St Paul's Cathedral to officers such as Rodney, Nelson, Howe and Collingwood. In keeping with the fact that he had died at home and had never gained the status of a national hero, it is relatively modest, and the trophies sketched by Soane in an early scheme, encouraged by Lady Bridport (XIII.1), were not executed. The inscription stated that the reader should:

> *For His Bravery, for his Abilities / For his Achievements in his Profession / For his Attachment to his King, and his Country, / Consult the annals of the British Navy, / Where they are written in Indelible Characters.*
>
> *Let this Monument record his private virtues. / He was a sincere and pious Christian, / A faithful and Affectionate Husband, / A Warm and*

Steady Friend to Merit / Benevolent to the Brave and Virtuous in Distress: / Kind to his Domestics, and Dependents, / The Patron of unprotected Youth, / The Poor Man's Benefactor, the Seamens' Friend, / Beloved, Revered, and Deplored by All.

Lady Bridport played an active part in the development of the design, a relatively involved process. As she put it to Soane, she was concerned to have 'the whole executed with the strictest propriety'. Patron and client met in London while the tomb was being designed, and Soane seems also to have assisted his friend in the administration of her husband's money.

The design developed by stages. Firstly Basevi drew up six designs for modest tablets from Soane's repertoire developed for the Newland, Bosanquet and de Loutherbourg tombs. These were delivered in December 1814 to Lady Bridport's agent. The following month Lady Bridport commented cautiously that the designs were 'all rather plain, but any one of them, when executed will I hope look well, and handsome, which is what I wish'.

Soane re-designed the wall monument in the form of a sarcophagus surmounted by a scrolled finial and submitted it in May 1815. Lady Bridport replied that it was 'a design, which as a drawing I greatly admire, but I am not certain that when executed for the Church, it would quite meet my Ideas...'.

In January 1816 Soane visited Cricket St Thomas and on his return to London began work on a more three-dimensional design. He first turned to a 1786 drawing of a design for Claude Bosanquet's monument (XIII.1) which he embellished with naval motifs. These included the transformation of the lateral elements into rostral columns, and the addition of banners which possibly referred to the French flags captured by Bridport during his naval service. The symbolism here included the familiar serpent of eternity. A drawing also executed in January 1816 (XIII.2)

XIII.1

XIII.2

showed alternative schemes for the sarcophagus for the patron's consideration.

The final stage (February–March 1816) reflected the private nature of the commission. It involved three variants on the theme of an Ionic aedicule on a sarcophagus, mounted on a block of Devonshire marble. They illustrate the concern to situate the monument so as to gain the most dramatic lighting effect: the drawings contrast the theatrically lit monument with the surrounding darkness, an effect which Soane often had his pupils convey in drawings of his tombs but which was difficult to capture in reality. XIII.4, a presentation drawing, differs from such a contemporary variant as XIII.3 primarily in the arrangement of the heraldic devices, to which Lady Bridport gave much thought.

The monument was executed by Thomas Grundy, two of whose masons travelled to Cricket to spend nine days fixing the monument. The total cost was £301.14.4., including a £15 fee for Soane.

XIII.1 *Elevation of a wall monument taking the form of an Ionic aedicule mounted upon a sarcophagus, with scale, a sketch plan and other designs*

This elevation is copied to scale, with slight amendments, from a 1786 Bosanquet design. It has been altered by the addition of naval trophies and the creation of rostral columns through the insertion of ships' prows.

Pen and coloured wash, with pencil additions (430 × 340)

SM 63/6/52

XIII.2 *Sketch of elevation, in Soane's hand, illustrating alternative forms of sarcophagus*

The drawing is inscribed with comments on the marble in Soane's hand, and dated January 1816. On the left, the sarcophagus widens towards its base and its lid is decorated with a Pompeian scroll. On the right, the tablet narrows towards its base, and a lion is perched on top.

Pen and pencil (520 × 370)

SM 63/6/59

104

XIII.3 *Elevation for presentation to Lady Bridport*

The drawing is inscribed as intended for Lady Bridport and dated 6 February 1816.

Pen and watercolour (545 × 425)

SM 63/6/67

XIII.4 *Perspective of design as executed*

The final design is based on XIII.3, with some alterations such as the new course of strigillation, the repositioning of the heraldic ornaments, and new heraldic details as suggested by Lady Bridport. Bridport's crest of a gull and anchor, surmounted by the coronet and a ribbon bearing the motto STEADY, tops the pediment. His coat-of-arms is supported by those of his two wives.

Pen, pencil and watercolour (505 × 460)

SM 63/6/69

Lemuel Francis Abbott (1760–1803)
XIII.5 *Alexander Hood, first Viscount Bridport,* 1795

At least three portraits survive of Bridport. In 1764 a three-quarter length portrait in the heroic style was painted by Sir Joshua Reynolds: this work was presented by his widow to the Painted Hall at Greenwich, which was then installed as a memorial of naval achievement. This half-length portrait (engraved in 1834) was the work of an artist with a particular enthusiasm for naval portraits, who painted Lord Hood as well as several studies of Nelson.

Oil (759 × 633)

National Portrait Gallery, London

XIII.6 *Letter from Lady Bridport to Sir John Soane*

In this letter dated '19th March 1816' Lady Bridport advises the architect on the 'Crest and Coronet', urging that she is anxious 'to have the whole executed with the strictest propriety'. On the facing page are sketches of the arms.

Ink on paper and wax seals (225 × 370)

SM Priv. Corr. XIII.H.27

XIV

Soane Family Tomb, 1816

Burial ground of St Giles-in-the Fields, now St Pancras'
Fields, London

*Sir John Soane's Museum: 43 drawings including site
plan, preliminary designs, and topographical views of
the tomb*

XIV.1

Mrs. Soane died in the early hours of 22 November 1815. Soane's Notebook remained blank until 1 December: 'The burial of all that is dear to me in this world, and all I wished to live for!' She was buried in the recently opened Old St Giles' Burial Ground, then on the northern outskirts of London.

Soane appears to have started work on the design on 11 February, with the office, especially Henry Parke and George Basevi, working on the project from mid-February to April. At this stage, Soane envisaged a structure (XIV.1) that would be open yet protected, with a central marble cube offering four faces for dedicatory inscriptions, enclosed by a marble canopy supported on four Ionic columns. Each face is almost identical to the Bridport monument. The delicate marble of the aedicule is in deliberate contrast to the primitive canopy. In the second stage the canopy structure is finalised, with the dome embellished by symbolism including the pineapple and serpent (XIV.2). At an early stage, Soane envisaged defining the boundary of the family plot by a low wall: this became a balustrade, with the canopy raised on a plinth. In the final stage, the protective screen was emphasised by abstract ornamentation particular to Soane and, as Summerson has suggested, possibly based on the Roman decorations discovered in the grounds of the Villa Negroni.

As the design approached completion, the pupils depicted the monument in various landscape settings, all suggesting poetic isolation rather than the bare cemetery.

Soane exhibited two views of the monument at the Royal Academy spring exhibition. He wrote in his Notebook on 26 April 'Private View of Exhib: but I cannot go! Alas poor Eliza, you always went thither on this day.' He had great difficulty in bringing himself to visit the site.

Soane's elder son John was buried there in 1823, and the architect himself in 1837. George was never admitted.

Designs for Public and Private Buildings, which appeared in 1828, concluded with this design. It was described as his '*Domus Aeterna*', in contrast to his 'temporary domicile' in Lincoln's Inn Fields. In Lecture IV Soane had written 'Many of these ancient tombs are in the form of a House because they considered this kind of Monument as a dwelling which was to have no end, and they therefore designated such tombs by the names of everlasting dwellings...'.

The monument has endured much hardship since Soane's day. In the Victorian period, it was affected by the railway cutting through to St Pancras. In 1869 continuing damage prompted the Trustees of Sir John Soane's Museum to write to the Parish, who suggested that the monument be moved to the safety of the Museum. It was repaired in 1919. In 1924 it probably served as the inspiration to Sir Giles Gilbert Scott in his design for the K 2 telephone kiosk.

In 1991 the monument was restored by the Soane Monuments Trust. It has since again been vandalised.

XIV.1 *Preliminary design*

This design shows a version of the first stage: a primitivist domed canopy on four piers encloses an Ionic aedicule.

Pencil and coloured washes (435 × 370)

SM 63/7/26

XIV.2 *Preliminary design: Elevation of aedicule and canopy, with sketches in margin*

The drawing is signed and dated 14 February 1816. On the verso Soane has sketched other details of the tomb.

Pen, pencil and coloured washes (535 × 370)

SM 63/7/3

XIV.3 *Perspective*

This view by Henry Parke is the first in a series of views made by the office showing progress on construction of the tomb. It is inscribed 'The monument as it appeared on Good Friday 12 April 1816'. The aedicule, pedestal and three of the four piers of the canopy have been erected.

Pencil, pen and ink, and watercolour (250 × 340)

SM 63/7/7

XIV.4 *Perspective*

The drawing shows the lid of the canopy in place. It is inscribed 'View of the Monument as it appeared on Saturday 13th of April at Midday'.

Watercolour (255 × 320)

SM 63/7/9

XIV.3

XIV.4

XIV.5

XIV.6

XIV.7

XIV.5 *Perspective*

This view from the north-west shows the monument surrounded by scaffolding and the finial being hoisted into position by a pulley and windlass.

Pencil and coloured washes (270 × 380)

SM 63/7/10

XIV.6 *Perspective*

This view from the south-west, dated 15 April, shows the two dice being delivered to the site and the first pieces of the stone kerb around the monument being laid.

Pencil, pen and ink, and watercolour (220 × 330)

SM 63/7/11

XIV.7 *Perspective*

This view from the north-west, dated 17 April, shows the masonry surround under construction; the old church of St Pancras is in the background.

Pencil, pen and ink, and watercolour (180 × 260)

SM 63/7/13

XIV.8 *Perspective*

This drawing depicts a harrowing but unexecuted scheme to carve a skeleton hurling a spear on the tomb's fourth face, which is implicitly dedicated to George, inflicter of Mrs Soane's 'Death Blows'. The fourth face in fact remains blank, as George was never admitted.

Pencil, pen and ink, and bodycolour (665 × 970)

SM 14/4/8 (Illustrated on front cover)

XIV.9 *Inscription for tomb of Mrs Soane*

These verses were written by Mrs Hofland, Soane's close friend, and were both engraved on the tomb and printed.

Printed paper (320 × 190)

SM 63/7/A

𝕾𝖆𝖈𝖗𝖊𝖉

TO THE MEMORY OF

ELIZABETH,

THE *WIFE OF* **JOHN SOANE**, ARCHITECT.

She died the 22d November, 1815.

WITH DISTINGUISHED TALENTS SHE UNITED AN AMIABLE AND AFFECTIONATE HEART.
HER PIETY WAS UNAFFECTED, HER INTEGRITY UNDEVIATING.
HER MANNERS DISPLAYED ALIKE DECISION AND ENERGY, KINDNESS, AND SUAVITY.
THESE, THE PECULIAR CHARACTERISTICS OF HER MIND, REMAINED UNTAINTED BY AN EXTENSIVE INTERCOURSE WITH THE WORLD.

Stranger——

If Virtue o'er thy Bosom bear Control;
If thine the gen'rous, thine th' exalted Soul;
Stranger, approach—this consecrated Earth
Demands thy Tribute to departed Worth:
Beneath this Tomb thy kindred Spirit sleeps,
Here Friendship sighs—here fond Affection weeps—
Here to the Dust Life's dearest Charm resign'd,
Leaves but the Dregs of ling'ring Time behind:
Yet one bright Ray to light the Grave is giv'n,
The Virtuous die not—they survive in Heav'n.

XIV.9

XIV.10 *Perspective*

This drawing depicts the family tomb in an imaginary setting, with Rousseau's tomb in the background.

Watercolour (705 × 1030)

SM 14/4/9

XV

Monument to Anna Storace, 1817

St Mary's, Lambeth, London (formerly Lambeth Parish Church; now Museum of Garden History)

Sir John Soane's Museum: no drawings

One of the most famous singers and actresses of her day, Anna Storace (1766–1817) led a vigorous and cosmopolitan life, which included an extended stay in Vienna, where she became the city's most admired soprano as well as the Emperor's mistress. She was the original Susanna in Mozart's *Marriage of Figaro* and the composer is said to have been in love with her. Storace returned to England in 1787 and continued to work in London and on the Continent until her retirement (long overdue in the opinion of some of her contemporaries, since she had become large and coarse-featured, while persisting in playing parts too young for her) in 1808, when she moved to the blameless residence of Herne Hill Cottage, Dulwich. Soane first saw her on stage when he was a student in Rome, and was captivated by her. When in London, she was a friend of the Soanes and is recorded in 1804 as dining at Lincoln's Inn Fields in the company of de Loutherbourg and Francis Bourgeois. Her nephew Brinsley Storace worked between 1804 and 1807 in Soane's office but was dismissed for idleness.

In September 1818 Mrs. Storace's mother wrote to Soane: 'I took the trouble to go over to Lambeth to see the Monument or Tablet you were so kind to undertake for me for my dear departed daughter. I was sorry to see it plac'd so immoderately high – 'twas so in the Extreme! – perfectly unnecessarily so, as there was plenty of room.' She felt it should be placed 'at least a foot lower' and in better light.

The design of the monument is close to that of Abraham Newland, but in its present form is without the Newland base or the acroteria, which may have been removed if the monument was moved within the church. The inscription was written by Prince Hoare, playwright and painter.

John Condé (d. 1794) after Samuel De Wilde (1748–1832)

XV.1 *Anna Storace,* 1791

Engraving (323 × 234)

National Portrait Gallery, London

XVI.1

XVI

Cenotaph to William Pitt, National Debt Redemption Office, 1818–20

Old Jewry, London; destroyed 1900

Sir John Soane's Museum: Over 60 drawings of designs for the National Debt Redemption Office, including a number for the Pitt Cenotaph

William Pitt the Younger (1759–1806) became Prime Minister at the age of 24. It was during his last ministry that the victory at Trafalgar took place, but the news shortly afterwards of Napoleon's victory at Austerlitz ('Roll up that map' he said 'It will not be needed these ten years') is said to have been his death blow. He was buried in Westminster Abbey and Parliament's Committee of Taste commissioned a monument there from Richard Westmacott.

In 1801, a group of City merchants had collected funds for a Pitt monument to commemorate his success as Chancellor of the Exchequer. One of his actions had been to establish, in 1786, a 'sinking' fund for the reduction of National Debt. By 1817 the fund required a larger office, and a site was acquired near the Bank of England. After Soane had begun to design the office, it was decided to include a statue of Pitt, probably using the money raised in the earlier subscription. Pitt had been a client and close acquaintance of Soane, and had secured his appointment as architect to the Bank of England. Soane's cenotaph design was inspired by gratitude to Pitt as a friend and as a national hero.

The effect of the two-storey top-lit tribune recalls the Dome at Lincoln's Inn Fields. A tribune was originally a raised platform from which a Roman magistrate dispensed justice: such structures were also erected to commemorate Roman emperors. The Corinthian Order was appropriate to elevated public figures.

A visitor to the Office would pass from the street into the hall and see the figure, lit from an invisi-ble source. Strangely, the statue shared the circulation space with the officials: the two upper storeys were the Principal's private rooms.

Westmacott's statue of Pitt was cast in bronze and depicted him in the dress of a Roman statesman, seated in a chair loosely derived from ancient Greek thrones. The statue survives at Pembroke College, Cambridge.

XVI.1 *Preliminary design: sectional perspective*

The cenotaph to William Pitt is seen from the public hall of the Office. The artist has chosen a low viewpoint, and his use of a sectional perspective is an ingenious way of depicting Soane's favourite device of a top-lit tribune. He draws with a strong sense of line, emphasising the structure rather than contrasts of light and shade.

This design dates from around January 1818. A statue of Britannia is placed in Pitt's chair.

Watercolour (1090 × 710)

SM 14/4/13

XVI.2 *Model of Pitt Cenotaph at final design stage*

By the spring Soane had significantly changed the design: this is the third of three models and is almost exactly as planned. The upper storey of the tribune is now detached from the surrounding structure and the illumination of the statue is more subtle and indirect. Pitt's chair is pushed into the shadow of the end bay, with a balustrade round the podium; the skylight is closed and lighting provided by clerestory windows. Alternate blind windows emphasise Soane's careful limitation of light.

A view in Britton's *The Union of Architecture, Painting and Sculpture* of 1827 shows the model placed above the doorway of Monk's Parlour, its hinges opened for dramatic effect.

Wooden scale model, enclosing a plaster model of Westmacott's design (730 × 600 × 460)

SM MR 58/214

XVIIc.1

XVII

Unexecuted Schemes

XVIIa   THE JAMES KING MAUSOLEUM, 1777

In his *Memoirs* Soane recalled his escape from a 'watery grave' 60 years before. He had agreed to celebrate a 21st birthday with two friends from the Royal Academy one Sunday in June 1776. Sunday was, however, the only day when a pupil was free, and he decided to stay at home to work on his design for the Royal Academy's Gold Medal. The two friends went to Greenwich and hired a boat. It overturned and James King, who could not swim, was drowned. Soane could not swim either, and if he had not stayed at his drawing-board would also have drowned.

A few months later, Soane's design for a *Triumphal Bridge* won the Gold Medal and a scholarship to study in Italy, which he described as 'the most fortunate event of my life'.

Before he went to Italy he designed this mausoleum, described by Summerson as in the nature of a 'funeral elegy'. He exhibited one design at the Royal Academy in 1777 and published a less ambitious version in 1778 in *Designs in Architecture*.

XVIIb   MAUSOLEUM TO THE EARL OF CHATHAM, 1778

William Pitt the Elder (1708–78) rallied Britain to a triumphant victory in the Seven Years' War, establishing the nation as a leading power. He died on 11 May 1778 and the following day Parliament voted for his burial in Westminster Abbey. The body lay in state until 9 June when it was borne, under banners, to the Abbey. He is commemorated there by a colossal marble monument sculpted by John Bacon, costing £6,000. Statues were also erected as far afield as New York and Charleston, South Carolina.

Soane had arrived in Rome on 2 May, and soon afterwards news of Chatham's death reached the English community there. Several English artists studying in Italy were moved to produce commemorative designs.

XVIIb.1   *Sectional elevation of the Chatham mausoleum, on a triangular plan, showing a sequence of top-lit rooms, with a central domed rotunda*

The design develops the James King mausoleum, removing the podium but introducing a triangular plan. The influence of Roman monuments is apparent: the shallow dome, lit through an oculus, recalls the Pantheon. Soane republished this design in *Sketches in Architecture* in 1793, in which it was described as a resting-place for 'great and virtuous characters', an early example of the theme of national commemoration.

Pen and watercolour (340 × 740)

SM 13/2/3

XVIIc   SEPULCHRAL CHURCH FOR WILLIAM PRAED, TYRINGHAM, 1799–1800

Tyringham, near Newport Pagnell, Buckinghamshire

In the 1790s Soane built a new country house, stables and a remarkable lodge (most of the buildings survive) for the banker William Praed. Construction finished in 1800, 'having engaged six of the most happy years of my life'. Soane enjoyed an excellent relationship with his client and later designed Praed's Bank in Fleet Street (now demolished).

Praed commissioned Soane to demolish the medieval church in the depopulated village and to design on the site an estate chapel, where the family would be interred and commemorated. The office worked on these designs during the winter of 1800–1, but the project was never executed.

The distinctive feature of the building is its triangular plan with the points terminated by rounded apses for the altar and private pews. The funerary character of the chapel is more boldly expressed in the exterior design: sarcophagi and cinerary urns surround the dome and an eternity serpent is coiled round the lantern.

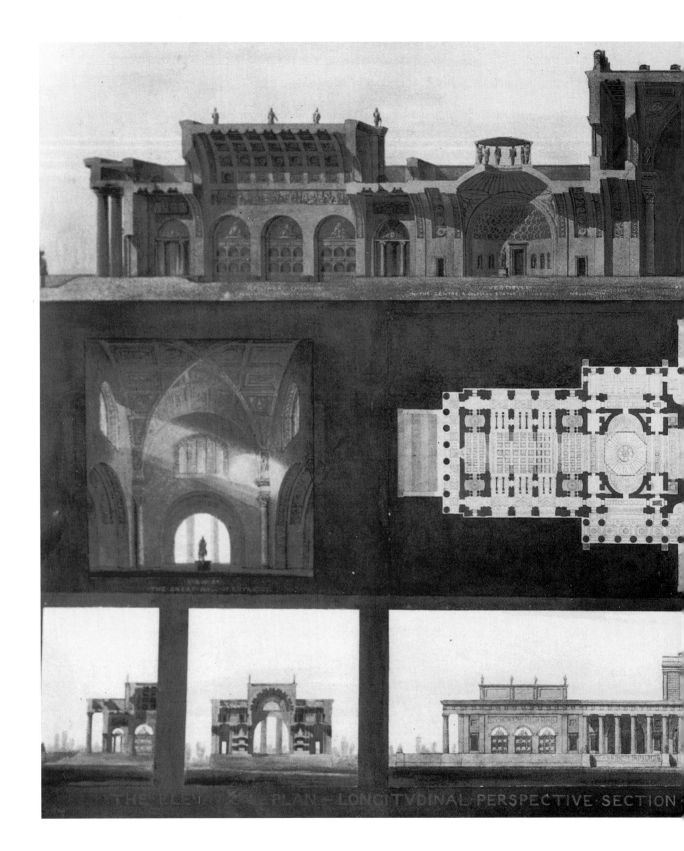

...OTHER PARTS OF A DESIGN FOR A NATIONAL MONVMENT . MDCCCXVIII.

J. M. Gandy RA

(with figures and amendments by A. van Assen)

XVIIc.1 *Preliminary design for Tyringham*

Gandy made several views of the chapel exterior, including a haunting scene set in moonlight (SM F96), one of which was exhibited at the Royal Academy in 1801 as a 'Sepulchral church'. This view was probably also intended for the spring exhibition.

This internal view was begun on 23 December 1800 and finished on 7 January 1801. Van Assen added, in addition to the figures, the pulpit and lectern and figures of saints in the niches. Gandy also made several views of the Chapel exterior.

Watercolour (710 × 660)

SM 13/5/7

XVIId DESIGN FOR A NATIONAL MONUMENT

As the Napoleonic Wars continued, awareness grew of the value of public commemoration of the fallen. Napoleon's glorification of Paris with monuments such as the Arc de Triomphe (begun in 1806) was an added incentive. After Waterloo, Parliament voted £300,000 for the erection of two monuments to express the nation's gratitude to its Army and Navy. 60 architects entered the competition, the winners being William Wilkins and Robert Smirke respectively. The money never materialised: as Wilkins commented in 1831, 'The nation's gratitude cooled'. The idea of such a commemoration persisted, however, and early schemes for the National Gallery's new building in Trafalgar Square included on the facade memorials of naval and military victory.

The competition encouraged Soane to design several memorials. This is one of eight 'National Monuments' displayed at the Royal Academy in 1818. It was described as 'a design to perpetuate the glorious achievements of British valour by sea and land'. Soane wished it to emulate the Pantheon in Paris.

In Soane's pantheon, the visitor ascended to a domed entrance hall containing an equestrian statue of George III. The hall led into two alternative symmetrical sequences of spaces, arranged on axis. On the left, the vestibule containing 'a colossal statue of the Duke of Wellington' led into a 'Sepulchral Chamber Dedicated to Military Glory'; on the right, a 'colossal statue of Lord Nelson' stands in the vestibule of 'a Sepulchral Chamber Dedicated to Naval Glory'. In the chambers, the visitor passed an array of cinerary urns, arranged in columbaria, and sarcophagi. In the Office Day Books the project was described as a 'mausoleum', suggesting Soane proposed to inter the actual remains of the fallen here, in addition to honouring their memory.

XVIId.1 *Design for a National Monument*

Soane prepared this drawing for the 1818 spring exhibition at the Royal Academy: during March, the pupil Edward Foxhall is recorded as 'Drawing designs of a mausoleum to a reduced scale'.

This composite image was an innovative method of presenting a complex design: precedents lie in French architectural drawings and textbooks.

A watercolour of 1825 shows that for a time Soane displayed the drawings in the Breakfast Parlour of 13 Lincoln's Inn Fields.

Nine individual watercolours, pasted on a sheet of shaded cardboard (730 × 1270)

SM 15/3/4

XVIIe DUKE OF YORK MONUMENT

Frederick Augustus, the 'Grand Old Duke of York' (1763–1827), was the second son of George III and Commander-in-Chief during the Napoleonic Wars. His career in battle was undistinguished but his administrative reforms were vital to Wellington's success and he gained reflected glory. Soane regarded this design as a national monument, describing it as a 'superb Sepulchral Church, with lofty Catacombs in the Construction of the Edifice', in which the nation's heroes would be interred.

The Duke died on 5 January 1827 and was buried at St George's, Windsor. On his own initiative, Soane made two commemorative schemes: a circular temple containing a colossal statue of the Duke and a sepulchral chapel. He proposed St James's Park as the location, opposite the Horse Guards, which had been the Duke's headquarters. The site was on the ceremonial route for the State

XVIIe.1

Opening of Parliament, the design for which dominated Soane's ambitions at this time. In *London and Westminster Improved* (1827) he envisaged a route from a new palace at Hyde Park Corner, down the Mall and into Whitehall via a triumphal arch at the entrance to Downing Street. This 'monument of national feeling and gratitude' would further embellish this sequence of patriotic symbols.

The design is a monumental version of the Tyringham chapel. The triangular plan is almost identical, with the principal portico aggrandised by an extra row of Grecian Doric columns appropriate to a temple honouring a warrior. The design is enriched by bombastic decorations: trophies, statues of soldiers and a railing composed of arrowheads. Sarcophagi are placed above the pediments, as at Tyringham. The shallow dome, based on the Pantheon, is surmounted by a colossal statue of the Duke.

In 1829 a subscription was raised for a monument to the Duke, to be placed in the position suggested by Soane. He was one of nine architects invited to submit designs. He did not submit this earlier design, accepting that its cost would exceed the £22,000 specified in the brief. The suc-

cessful architect was Benjamin Wyatt, who conformed to the Committee's recommendation of a single pillar with the dimensions of Trajan's Column. It stands at the head of Duke of York's Steps, surmounted by a bronze statue by Westmacott. Soane donated £1,000 to the cost of the bronze.

Soane never abandoned his commitment to a national monument: the last design on which he worked before his death was a monument to the Duke of Wellington.

J. M. Gandy
XVIIe.1 *Perspective view of the Duke of York Monument*

The drawing shows a military funeral in progress, with the Horse Guards in the background. It was accompanied at the 1828 Royal Academy exhibition by an internal view, also by Gandy, showing the coffin lying in state, and dated 12 December 1827. In 1837 the two drawings hung in the North Drawing Room of the Museum, where Soane assembled images of many of the monumental projects of his later years.

Watercolour (805 × 1040)

SM F110

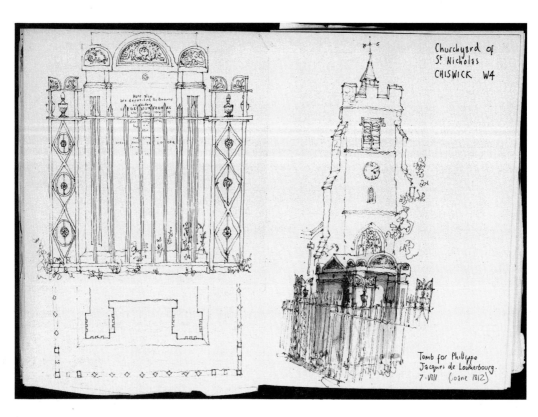

Churchyard of
St Nicholas
CHISWICK W4

Tomb for Philippe
Jacques de Loutherbourg.
7·VIII (done 1812)

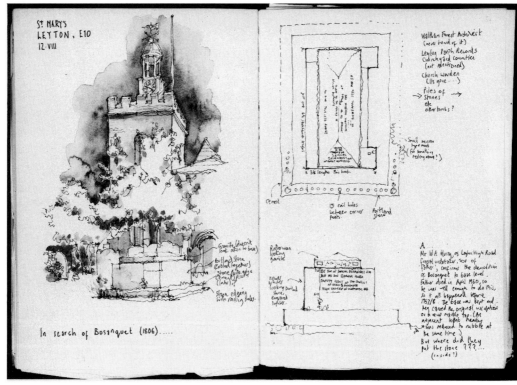

ST MARY'S
LEYTON, E10
12·VIII

In search of Bosanquet (1806).....

120

Ptolemy Dean

Monuments and Time

Soane's monuments have had the same varied fate as his buildings. One was lost in the London Blitz: the 1786 monument to Claude Bosanquet in the City church of St Stephen's, Coleman Street. Unfortunately it appears that any monuments that may have survived were cleared away with the rubble.

The tomb for Samuel Bosanquet (IX) was in the once-rural Leyton churchyard, now a part of the East End. Thought to have been lost entirely, its plinth can still be found under a c.1957 recarved granite top.

Elsewhere in London, things have been more fortunate. Soane's own tomb in Old St Pancras churchyard (XIV), the de Loutherbourg Tomb in Chiswick (XII), and the Johnston tomb in St Mary Abbot's churchyard Kensington (IV) have all recently been restored.

The Newland tablet in Southwark Cathedral (XI), the only monument actually signed by Soane, survives with cement repairs presumably from wartime bomb damage. The Storace tablet (XV) in St Mary's church, upstream in Lambeth, is almost identical, except it has lost both pediment and plinth. This might have occurred when the tablet was relocated within the church during the nineteenth century.

Outside of London, Soane's column to Michael Hills (VII) still rises unexpectedly from some fields in Essex and has recently regained its urn, whilst the Evelyn Monument (V), relocated from Surrey to Northumberland in 1928, is magnificently sited with the Cheviot Hills beyond. It is this very exposure which has worsened problems of rusting cramps in the stonework. These pieces of iron that tie the stones together expand to seven times their original volume, and blow off the face

Mr Hurry with the remains of Samuel Bosanquet's monument; Mr Hurry remembers his father, whose undertaker's business he now runs, demolishing the tomb.

of the stonework.

The monument to the second Baron Lyttelton (1808), illustrated in Joseph Michael Gandy's famous fantasy of all Soane's works up to 1815, lost its urn in the nineteenth-century reconstruction of Hagley Church, Worcestershire, although the inscribed marble plaque (with its edges chipped and damaged from the move) still survives. Soane had allowed a weekend to visit it in 1808, but wrote that 'two or three hours will, I presume, be sufficient to do all that I have to do to the Monument'.

The memorial to Viscount Bridport at Cricket St Thomas (XIII) has survived the Victorian reconstruction of that church, but the church itself is now rather ignominiously within the Noel Edmonds' Crinkly Bottom Theme Park. Things in Reading are little better: the Simeon Monument (VIII) has been engulfed by heavy Victorian railings and the town's public conveniences.

A number of other monuments survive which are thought to be by Soane. There are the three tablets in the transepts of Wardour Castle Chapel, which Soane extended for Lord Arundell in 1788. Each tablet is of white marble with a flush inset border of pink marble around the edge, very similar in spirit to the Newland and Storace tablets. John Patterson's tablet in St Peter Mancroft, Norwich (1833) also has a Soanean appearance. Soane had carried out alterations to Patterson's Norwich house in 1790, and Patterson continued a correspondence with Soane until his death. Soane may have provided a design for the tablet and not kept a copy.

Soane did record sending four designs for an obelisk to a General Murray in 1790, but the rather coarsely detailed and tooled granite obelisk that survives at Beauport (Murray's house on the outskirts of Hastings) is dated 1812 and lacks the presence of Soane's other monuments. The Raikes mausoleum at Woodford in Essex (1800) is a much more sophisticated construction, but again, there is insufficient evidence firmly to determine Soane's contribution.

The author is the Soane Monuments Trust Fellow

Appendix

'The last testament of Sir Francis Bourgeois'

Manuscript in Sir John Soane's Museum reproduced by courtesy of The Trustees of the Museum
Ref: Private Correspondence IX/D/2/2

On the day of Decr. 1810 Corry called upon me at my Chambers in the Temple, & told me Sir Francis Bourgeois had been exceedingly ill, & that he had seen him I think the day before, when Sir Francis, declared to him his intention of leaving Dulwich College his Collection of Pictures, & that he had made him & Mr Greenwell the Solicitor, his Executors. I said I hoped he had given him a good Legacy, he told me he had left him & Mr Greenwell 1000 each. He asked me what I thought of the business, I told him nothing could give me greater pleasure, & that I would do every thing I possibly could to give effect to his intentions, & that if he thought right he might assure Sir Francis of it. I think he told me, that Sir Francis's Heart was in this business, & He was sure He would be pleased to hear this circumstance, when, I believe, I said that if it would be any satisfaction to him, I should be ready to give him my assurance of it. – This was related to Sir Francis Bourgeois about a week afterwards who expressed a wish to see me at his House, at Eleven oclock the following day, to meet Corry & Mr Greenwell, when I went there, I arrived before them, & was admitted in to him. He seemed a good deal pulled down by his disorder, the leg seemed swelled, & it was upon a stool, but he seemed in other respects chearful & lively. He almost immediately began to speak on the subject, about which He had wished to see me, and which he open'd with considerable earnestness, & vivacity. From his manner & tone of voice I thought him considerably better, than I had been led to expect, indeed he appeared to me by no means in any immediate danger. He told me that he supposed I had heard of the subject on which he wished to see me, & I told him I had, He said he wished the Collection of Pictures to go down to Posterity just as it was, that this object had perpetually occupied his mind, I think He said that many persons had talked to him about this Collection of Pictures, & amongst others Lord Buckinghamshire, who said come along with me to the British Museum. We will look over it, & see their regulations. He said He went there with him, but that it was an unfortunate thing for them, that he was shewn their rules, for that He did not approve of them, He said He was an Aristocrat both in feeling & principle, that he had always been so, that He had the highest respect for the Aristocracy everywhere, except in the Arts, that the Governors excercised an Aristocracy which He did not approve of, in the right of putting up, & taking down, & getting rid of any thing they might choose, for instance he said they have the right of disposing of a Picture for a Stove. I met William Smith he said, I think at the dinner given by the Royal Academy, who asked him what he had a mind to do with his Pictures, I asked him what have <u>you</u> a mind to do, when Wm Smith said if you will give a certain number to the Public I will do the same, come I said that is fair. – I think but am not sure, that Sir Francis said, He did not approve of Mr Smiths plan, but the exact reasons I do not recollect, but believe it was because he still disapproved of the British Museum. He then said He had an idea of getting the House where He lived, made freehold & had applied to the Duke of Portland, who had made some difficulties, He therefore gave up the plan He had of making a Gallery there, After considering all these things in his mind, & wishing that the Collection, should go down to Posterity for the benefit of the Public, & thinking how it might best be done, He was better satisfied with the unpretending merit of Dulwich College, than with these great institutions, & had come to the resolution of leaving the whole to them. – He said in doing so, He meant that his Collection of Pictures should go down whole to Posterity, That if Mr Desenfans could put his Head out of the Grave He might be able to see them as much as possible in the same state as he left them in, He said therefore he would give the Furniture of the Skylight room, together with the China some of which was valuable, He said it may appear frivolous at such a time my making any mention of a subject so trifling as a dinner, but I should wish that a handsome dinner was given once a year to the President of the Royal Academy & one or two Persons skilled in the Arts, who would point out what Pictures wanted cleaning. This Dinner to be the Dinner of the Master Warden & Fellows & to be their invitation "I have a Service of Plate plates & all (I think he said) for six and thirty people, which I shall give you also" He said it would be necessary to provide proper persons to look after & to shew the Pictures, & he asked me what I would suggest upon that point, I told him that He was a much better judge, than I could possibly be, He said Two men would be necessary, & asked what should be the Wages of the 1st. When I said I thought it ought to be something more than the Wages of a Gentlemans Butler. He said yes, <u>that</u> is right, suppose we say 100 a year I said yes, I thought this would do, the 2d man He said ought to have 80, I said dont you think that is too much for the 2d? & I think he said He ought to have 70. He said from long experience I know pretty well what will be the expence on the average of having them cleaned, it will be about 100 a year. He then said How much is that? & upon being told, He said What Sum will be necessary out of which to raise a fund for this purpose, I think he mentioned the dinner to be paid for out of this, but I do not recollect that he mentioned any thing else, & without I believe any sum being stated, He said £10,000. He desired (I should say that Mr Greenwell and Corry joined us after I had been there about 20 minutes, I should think we were with him about 2 hours) Mr Greenwell to take down on Paper his instructions for the purpose of being witnessed & signed as his Will, in case he had no opportunity of putting them more at length. He then asked me on what terms the Pictures ought to be shewn, I said I thought that a matter of very serious consideration & I could then hardly tell on what terms they ought to be shewn, I said I was not sure that for the convenience of the Public, the terms ought not to be pecuniary, but that I had not made up my mind, He said He thought so too, but he was of opinion that the sum ought not to be a high one, & I said most certainly and I believe the particular words in Sir Francis Will, "upon such terms pecuniary or otherwise" were of my suggestion. He said you may make a considerable sum I said it was by no means with a view of that kind that I mentioned it, "or, said He, it might be given to some of the Poorer part of your Society," when Corry said, they were exceedingly well off already, I think He said, "very well," I wont interfere with that", but I am pretty sure he immediately gave up his suggestion. Now he said in respect to a place to hold them, you have already a Fund for rebuilding your Picture Gallery, & you mean to enlarge your Chapel, We said yes, He said How much will it take to rebuild the Gallery & West Wing? I believe Corry said He thought it would take £4000. When Sir Francis said I will meet you half way, & give £2000, it was stated at the time that the enlargement of the Chapel would cost a considerable Sum, & I think He said, He meant afterwards to appropriate something specific for that purpose. He said He wished that Mr Desenfans's Body might be removed there, & it was his wish, that He, & he knew it was Mrs Desenfans wish, to be removed there into a little part of the Chapel which He would provide for, We told him yes by all means – He said Mr Desenfans had a sort of prejudice against being put under ground, & he should therefore like some little nook of the chapel, to be set apart, that instead of being buried under ground, the Bodies should be placed in Sarcophagi which, I think he said, He would undertake to provide, upon my asking what sort of Sarcophagui He meant, he said such as were in his Chapel, & on finding I had never been in the Chapel, or indeed heard of it, He desired me to walk & look at it, saying that Soane had built it out of a Coach House 25ft long I think. – I returned & said I thought it very beautiful. Now He said when you make any alterations, how do you mean to have them done? I said I was of opinion that for establishments such as ours, the Gothic was clearly the Style, He said yes most certainly, He said whom do you mean to employ? I said whom do you recommend? He said what do you think of Soane, I said we should undoubtedly pay every attention to his wish, but asked him if Mr Soane did not always object to do any thing in the Gothic Style, He said He does in general, but your Chapel is built by Inigo Jones & He is one of his most enthusiastic admirers, I said in that case we should be most happy to take any recommendation of his, He said when I get better I will come down to you & we will look to all these things, He said Soane is a man of Fortune has only two Sons who will be most amply provided for, I think he said you may depend upon his treating you as a friend, & that He will not make it an expensive business & Said, if I remember right, that He gave him a carte blanche as to his Chapel, that the Estimate was £600 & that he built it for about £580, I do not now recollect that he said any thing more about the business. Mr Greenwell by his desire, took down Memorandums which he desired him to put into form immediately for him to witness, as it was his wish that if he was carried off suddenly his intentions might be complied with. – He seemed to be in some pain so I thought it right to shorten my visit, so after assuring him again that I would endeavour to the best of my power conscientiously to discharge any trust he might repose in me, & hoping to see him again very soon able to go about, I wished him good morning, & never saw him afterwards –

LB Allen

A NOTE ON 'THE LAST TESTAMENT OF SIR FRANCIS BOURGEOIS'

This memorandum was written by Lancelot Baugh Allen, Master of Dulwich College from 1811 to 1820. The Revd. Robert Corry was usher at Dulwich College from 1806 to 1812 and a close friend of Bourgeois. The fourth Earl of Buckinghamshire (1760–1816), a politician with strong Irish connections, served briefly under William Pitt the Younger, through whose friendship with Soane he may have met Bourgeois. William Smith MP (1756–1835), also a politician and a member of the radical Clapham Sect, was a collector of paintings and a patron of living artists: he owned at one time the prime version of Reynolds's *Mrs Siddons as the Tragic Muse* of which Desenfans commissioned the second version.

Dulwich College and Picture Gallery, 1819

Bibliography

TEXTS RELATING TO SOANE

ANDREW BALLANTYNE, 'First Principles and Ancient Errors: Soane at Dulwich', *Architectural History*, 37, 1994

ARTHUR T. BOLTON, ed., *Description of the House and Museum on the North Side of Lincoln's Inn Fields, the Residence of Sir John Soane*, Oxford 1920

ARTHUR T. BOLTON, ed., *The Portrait of Sir John Soane, R. A. (1753–1837) Set forth in Letters from his Friends*, London 1927

ARTHUR T. BOLTON, ed., *The Lectures on Architecture of Sir John Soane*, London 1929

HELEN DOREY, 'Soane's Acquisition of the Sarcophagus of Seti I', *Georgian Group Journal*, 1991

JOHN FLAXMAN, *Lectures on Sculpture*, London 1829, pp. 1–2

PETER GUILLERY, 'Norwood Hall and Micklefield Hall: Works by Sir John Soane', *Architectural History*, 30, 1987

JOHN HARRIS, *Sir William Chambers: Knight of the Polar Star*, London 1970

BRIAN LUKACHER, *Joseph Michael Gandy: The Poetical Representation and Mythography of Architecture*, Ph.D. thesis, University of Delaware 1987

BRIAN LUKACHER, 'Phantasmagoria and Emanations: Lighting Effects in the Architectural Fantasies of Joseph Michael Gandy', *Architectural Association Files*, 4, 1983, pp. 40–48

G.-TILMAN MELLINGHOFF, 'Soane's Dulwich Picture Gallery *Revisited*' in *John Soane*, Architectural Monographs, London 1983

SUSAN FEINBERG MILLENSON, *Sir John Soane's Museum*, Michigan 1987

PIERRE DE LA RUFFINIÈRE DU PREY, *John Soane: The Making of an Architect*, Chicago and London 1982

JOHN SOANE, *Designs in Architecture*, London 1778

JOHN SOANE, *Sketches in Architecture*, London 1793

JOHN SOANE, *Designs for Public and Private Buildings*, London 1828

JOHN SOANE, *Memoirs of the Professional Life of an Architect between the years 1768 and 1835 written by Himself*, London 1835

JOHN SOANE, *Description of the House and Museum etc*, enlarged edition, London 1835

DOROTHY STROUD, *The Architecture of Sir John Soane*, 1961 and 1983

JOHN SUMMERSON, 'Sir John Soane and the furniture of death', *Architectural Review*, March 1978

JOHN SUMMERSON, *The Unromantic Castle*, London 1990

PETER THORNTON AND HELEN DOREY, *A Miscellany of Objects from Sir John Soane's Museum*, London 1992

GILES WATERFIELD, *Soane and After: The Architecture of Dulwich Picture Gallery*, Dulwich Picture Gallery, London 1987

DAVID WATKIN, 'Freemasonry and Sir John Soane', *Journal of the Society of Architectural Historians*, LIV, December 1995, pp. 2–17

DAVID WATKIN, *Sir John Soane: Enlightenment Thought and the Royal Academy Lectures*, Cambridge 1996

CONTEMPORARY THEORETICAL AND PHILOSOPHICAL TEXTS

JACQUES-FRANCOIS BLONDEL, *Cours d'architecture*, 9 vols., Paris 1771–7

GERMAIN BOFFRAND, *Livre d'architecture*, Paris 1745

EDMUND BURKE, *A Philosophical Enquiry into the Origin of our Ideas of the Sublime and Beautiful* (1757), London 1767

NICOLAS LE CAMUS DE MÉZIÈRES, *Le génie de l'architecture; ou, l'analogie de cet art avec nos sensations*, Paris 1780

WILLIAM CHAMBERS, *A Dissertation on Oriental Gardening*, London 1772

MARC-ANTOINE LAUGIER, *Observations sur l'architecture*, The Hague 1765

CLAUDE-NICOLAS LEDOUX, *Architecture considérée sous le rapport de l'art, des moeurs, et de la législation*, Paris 1804

ABBÉ CHARLES-FRANÇOIS DE LUBERSAC, *Discours sur les monumens publics de tous les âges*, Paris 1775

BERNARD DE MONTFAUCON, *L'Antiquité expliquée*, Paris 1719

PIERRE PATTE, *Monumens érigés en France à la gloire de Louis XVI*, Paris 1765

GIOVANNI BATTISTA PIRANESI, *Il Campo Marzio dell'antica Roma*, Rome 1762

CESARE RIPA, *Iconologia*, Rome 1603

A. SMITH, *The Theory of Moral Sentiments*, ed. D. D. Raphael and A. L. Macfie, Oxford 1979

JOHANN JOACHIM WINCKELMANN, *Histoire de l'art chez les anciens*, Yverdon 1784

GENERAL TEXTS

N. BARLEY, *Dancing on the Grave: Encounters with Death*, London 1995

O. BLAND, *The Royal Way of Death*, London, 1986

ROGER BOWDLER, 'Wisdom's School: London's pre-Victorian Cemeteries', *The London Gardener*, 1995

FREDERICK BURGESS, *English Churchyard Memorials*, 1963

MARIE BUSCO, *Sir Richard Westmacott, Sculptor*, Cambridge 1994

T. D. CAMPBELL, *Adam Smith's Science of Morals*, London 1971

R. CECIL, *A Friendly Visit to the House of Mourning*, London, no date

HOWARD COLVIN, *Architecture and the After-Life*, New Haven and London 1991

F. H. CROSSLEY, *English Church Monuments AD 1150–1550*, 1921

JAMES STEVENS CURL, *A Celebration of Death*, 1980

JAMES STEVENS CURL, *The Art and Architecture of Freemasonry: an Introductory Study*, 1991

JAMES STEVENS CURL, 'Young's *Night Thoughts* and the Origins of the Garden Cemetery', *Journal of Garden History*, 14, 2, Summer 1994

DONNA C. CURTZ AND JOHN BOARDMAN, *Greek Burial Customs*, 1971

MAURICE DAVIES, *Turner the Professor: The Artist and Linear Perspective*, Tate Gallery, London 1992

RICHARD A. ETLIN, *The Architecture of Death*, Cambridge, Mass., and London 1984

PHILIPP FEHL, *The Classical Monument: Reflections on the Connection between Morality and Art in Greek and Roman Sculpture*, New York 1972

M. M. GARLAND, 'Victorian Unbelief and Bereavement', in R. Houlbrooke, ed., *Death, Ritual and Bereavement*, London, 1989

RUPERT GUNNIS, *A Biographical Dictionary of British Sculptors 1660–1851*, 1954

FRANCIS HASKELL AND NICHOLAS PENNY, *Taste and the Antique*, New Haven and London, 1988

D. IRWIN, 'Sentiment and Antiquity: European Tombs, 1750–1830', in J. Whaley, ed., *Mirrors of Mortality: Studies in the Social History of Death*, London 1981

ALISON KELLY, *Mrs Coade's Stone*, Upton-on-Severn 1990

DAVID KING, *The Complete Works of Robert and James Adam*, 1991

JULIAN LITTEN, *The English Way of Death*, 1991

N. LLEWELLYN, '"Plinie is a weghtye witnesse": The Classical Reference in Post-Reformation Funeral Monuments' in Lucy Gent, ed., *Albion's Classicism: The Visual Arts in Britain 1550-1660*, 1995, pp. 147–162

ALLAN I. LUDWIG, *Graven Images*, Middletown, Ct. 1966

JEAN-MARIE PÉROUSE DE MONTCLOS, 'Les Prix de Rome', *Concours de l'Académie royale d'architecture au XVIIIe siècle*, Paris 1984

J. MCMANNERS, *Death and the Enlightenment: Changing Attitudes to Death among Christian and Unbelievers in Eighteenth Century France*, Oxford 1981

NICHOLAS PENNY, *Church Monuments in Romantic England*, New Haven & London 1977

Remarks on English Churches, and on the Expediency of Rendering Sepulchral Memorials subservient to Pious and Christian Uses, Oxford 1842

E. SCHOR, *Bearing the Dead: The British Culture of Mourning from the Enlightenment to Victoria*, Princeton 1994

A. SKINNER, 'Introduction', in A. Smith, *The Wealth of Nations*, Harmondsworth, 1970

W. STROEBE AND M. S. STROEBE, *Bereavement and Health: The Psychological and Physical Consequences of Partner Loss*, Cambridge 1987

C. TOMALIN, *Mrs. Jordan's Profession: The story of a great actress and a future King*, London 1995

J.M.C. TOYNBEE, *Death and Burial in the Roman World*, 1971

Turner & Architecture, Tate Gallery, London 1988

MARGARET WHINNEY, *Sculpture in Britain 1530–1830* 2nd ed., 1988

BETTY WILLSHER AND DOREEN HUNTER, *Stones*, Edinburgh and Vancouver, 1978

JOHN WILTON-ELY, *The Mind and Art of Giovanni Battista Piranesi*, 1978

ALISON YARRINGTON, *The Commemoration of the Hero 1800–1864: Monuments to British Victors of the Napoleonic Wars*, (Ph.D. thesis, Cambridge 1980), New York and London 1988

Soane and Death: The Tombs and Monuments of Sir John Soane

Catalogue edited by Giles Waterfield

Designed by Barry Viney

© Dulwich Picture Gallery, London 1996

Photoset and printed in England by the Lavenham Press, Water Street, Lavenham, Suffolk, CO10 9RN

ISBN 1 898 519 08 0

This catalogue accompanies an exhibition held at Dulwich Picture Gallery, 29 February - 12 May 1996

PHOTOGRAPHIC CREDITS

Photographs are credited by kind permission of the owners and to the following:
Courtauld Institute   p. 20, fig. 2
English Heritage   p. 29, fig. 3; p. 42, fig. 15
Greater London Record Office   p. 39, fig. 13; p. 43, fig. 16
RCHME © Crown Copyright   p. 22, fig. 6

We are grateful to Geremy Butler at Sir John Soane's Museum; and to Stefan Buzas, Ian B. Jones and Ptolemy Dean.